Waking Up to Heal

to

Heal

Sharon Critchfield

BALBOA.
PRESS

A DIVISION OF HAY HOUSE

Balboa Press books may be ordered through booksellers or by contacting:

Balboa Press
A Division of Hay House
1663 Liberty Drive
Bloomington, IN 47403
www.balboapress.com
1 (877) 407-4847

Because of the dynamic nature of the Internet, any web addresses or links contained in this book may have changed since publication and may no longer be valid. The views expressed in this work are solely those of the author and do not necessarily reflect the views of the publisher, and the publisher hereby disclaims any responsibility for them.

The author of this book does not dispense medical advice or prescribe the use of any technique as a form of treatment for physical, emotional, or medical problems without the advice of a physician, either directly or indirectly. The intent of the author is only to offer information of a general nature to help you in your quest for emotional and spiritual well-being. In the event you use any of the information in this book for yourself, which is your constitutional right, the author and the publisher assume no responsibility for your actions.

Any people depicted in stock imagery provided by Thinkstock are models, and such images are being used for illustrative purposes only.
Certain stock imagery © Thinkstock.

Print information available on the last page.

ISBN: 978-1-5043-4450-0 (sc)
ISBN: 978-1-5043-4452-4 (hc)
ISBN: 978-1-5043-4451-7 (e)

Library of Congress Control Number: 2015918575

Balboa Press rev. date: 12/11/2015

This book is dedicated to everyone who is waking up to heal. It is about time. Reclaiming our spiritual identity and living with purpose, honoring our physical, emotional, mental, and spiritual bodies is everyone's calling.

You don't have a soul. You are a soul. You have a body.
— George MacDonald

How does one heal from unspeakable trauma? Is it even possible? Are there blessings to be found in even the most heinous experiences? Why do some people glide through traumatic life-altering events with no visible scars while others fall victim to depression and addiction? How does one come out on the other side a stronger and more compassionate person?

These are questions that every person asks at some point in his or her life. The answers are not elusive or mysterious, only to be answered when we die. There are answers available now, and there are productive ways to heal from any experience and learn valuable life lessons that will serve to make you a stronger and more complete soul.

CONTENTS

ACKNOWLEDGMENTS

First and foremost, I want to thank my husband, whose encouragement was my motivation to write this book. I thank him for his patience with me throughout the process. As I wrote this book, I realized that most of the material would not have been possible without him in my life. We held each other together through it all and make a pretty good team. He is also a closet editor, for which I am very thankful. I love you and thank God every day for sending you to me.

I want to thank my children for allowing me the privilege of being your mom. I am so proud of both of you. Shelley, thank you for your unending support and for being the voice of reason in every scheme I hatch. Matt, without your help, this book would only be a dream in my head, so thank you from the bottom of my heart. Ben, thank you for making my daughter the absolute happiest she has ever been in her life. Thank you for your invaluable and objective input that only made this book better.

I have to thank my sisters who have been with me even since before I was born. I appreciate the support you have given me, not only as I wrote this book, but throughout my whole life. I also cannot put into words how appreciative I am that you liked what I wrote.

I also thank Balboa Press for helping me get this story out there and making it all so easy.

Lastly, I wish to thank all the experts whom I have studied and all the wonderful books, courses, and other material they have made available for lightworkers like me.

INTRODUCTION

Healing doesn't mean the damage never existed. It means the damage no longer controls our lives.
—Akshay Dubey

Early on, I knew in my heart I was destined for something different than what I was currently doing. Something was calling to me, something spiritual in nature imploring me to wake up—to wake up to my spiritual purpose; wake up to the new beliefs I had been slowly forming; wake up to heal. I believe there are literally millions, if not more, people today who feel this same way and are either trying desperately to wake up or have already begun the process but don't know what to do next. My belief is that each of us has a plan put together for us by God. There are people for us to meet, synchronicities to act upon, lessons to learn, and successes to celebrate. Navigating this masterful plan enables us to become our authentic true selves.

This book is a culmination of my life events. Some are universal and quite ordinary. Some are comical, as only life could make them. Many are traumatic and tragic with a screaming and desperate cry for healing. My goal was to share how I healed and came out on the other side a stronger and more compassionate person. I found that it is possible to find blessings beneath the pain and there are lessons to be learned from each experience. My hope is that you see yourself in these pages and that what you see gives you hope and begins a journey of healing. Another goal of mine was to show how a conservative, evangelical family of the 60s that practiced religion as a life form and interpreted the Bible in the most literal of ways could produce a daughter who would grow up to realize her true gift was helping others to heal themselves holistically. This approach involves healing every aspect of all human experiences resulting in a more complete spiritual, mental, physical and emotional soul ready to evolve into a higher consciousness. What does it take to make that huge of a transformation? I believe it took every circumstance, loss, success, and challenge the universe threw my way to shape the person I am today.

Healing is integral to each of us and can be the sole purpose for some in this life. Healing does not only refer to our physical bodies, but also—and more importantly—includes our emotional, mental, and spiritual bodies. Healing can come in the form of a nature walk, a long-awaited hug, a call to help others, or a person who appears in your path to help show you the way. Healing can happen when you write, draw, create, forgive, and pray. Healing is not elusive; it is available to anyone willing to delve into those parts of them that need it the most.

My prayer is that the lessons your soul yearns to learn will be discovered in your life events so your soul can move forward on its journey. I wish you heartfelt blessings and I pray that all of your lessons are learned with a grateful heart. I believe if everyone in the world were to own their own awakening, the earth would be forever changed. Thank you for sharing my journey with me. I invite you to laugh with me, cry with me, and heal with me.

My spiritual awakening led me to some truths that have become the cornerstone for my healing. They are my foundations for living day-by-day on a spirit-filled journey of healing and transformational growth. It took me fifty-four years to establish this core belief system. I urge you to create or consider your own beliefs and how they can shape your future.

- There exists a universal power greater than all of us, and it connects us all. We are all one with this power some call

God, Creator, or the Almighty. No matter what you call this universal power, it does exist, and we are one with our Creator.

- Everything is energy. Everything. According to the laws of physics, energy cannot be created or destroyed, but it can be changed or converted. Energy in the body can be blocked causing illness but then unblocked to heal. It can be moved to enable us to achieve balance in our lives, and it can be a manifesting powerhouse when coupled with intention, emotion, and action.
- Everything is operating on a vibrational frequency. Each one of us has our own vibration, and it is ever changing with our moods, feelings, and thoughts. The higher our vibration, the more apt we are to manifest what we desire. Getting and maintaining that higher vibration becomes the daily challenge we all face.
- There are many ways to heal. They are not always easy, and it is ultimately up to the person to shape his or her own future. The difference between those who come out on the other side and those who succumb to depression and addiction is directly related to how much of an effort they put into their own healing. Some give up, and some carry on to spite the obstacles and the difficulty.
- Do not depend on another person for your own happiness. Self-love is perhaps the greatest lesson we are here on earth to learn.
- The earth has a collective consciousness, and it is ever changing. The vibration of individuals on the planet can raise the vibration of the planet as a whole, helping to foster the awakening of each person.
- We are never alone. There are multitudes of angels, guides, masters, and loved ones in spirit that are just waiting on us to ask them for help, and they are overjoyed when we do.
- All of us have an inner guidance system, and if we just listen to it, we can utilize it to make good decisions, avoid danger, and guide our daily lives. Intuition is clearly the

map for the journey I am on. It lets me know exactly where to go and how to get there.

- We are all on our own journeys, but those journeys are constantly changing. We are always seeking a higher level of understanding. What we learned previously is not wrong. We just advance in our learning and understanding of those truths. Your journey is your own and belongs to no one but you.

There is a voice inside you
That whispers all day long,
"I feel that this is right for me, I know that this is wrong."
No teacher, preacher, parent, friend or wise man can decide
What's right for you—just listen to the voice that speaks inside.
—Shel Silverstein

CHAPTER ONE

Man Cannot Live by Bread Alone

It's not our job to toughen our children up to face a cruel and heartless world. It's our job to raise children who will make the world a little less cruel and heartless.
—L. R. Knost

Suppose you were to sit down and write a chapter about your childhood. What would you say? Would it be revealing, emotional, and nostalgic, or would it bring back tough memories best forgotten? My effort was eye opening, to say the least. It brought some much-needed healing for me, and it can for anyone who dares to go back in time to where all the wounds began.

I grew up in a very strict, suburban, middle-class, evangelical American family with a stay-at-home mom and a working dad who stayed married and had three daughters. Sounds pretty good, doesn't it? Sounds like a typical American family of the 1960s. There is nothing bad or wrong with any of those adjectives just used to describe a family. However, every household has skeletons in the closet. In my family, the skeletons were not only in the closet; they were shaking their bones and hiding behind the clothes, trying bravely to wait it out and not be discovered. If you were to ask me if I thought I had a good upbringing or a good childhood, I would not even blink an eye to say yes, in spite of the crippling fear and anxiety I faced each and every day.

My dad was career military, honoring his country by serving in the navy from too young an age to witness the horrors of war. He was a Pearl Harbor survivor and has written a book about his life with a focus on his military career. As a child of a decorated war hero, I cannot dismiss this brave and honorable part of the man I called Daddy for most of my life. It was indeed a sacrifice for him to serve in this way, as it was for the rest of us at some point along the way. So I thank him for his service and bravery in so many years of war that would only end with the use of the atomic bomb.

My mom grew up in a poor household with two sisters and a brother. She was very close to her family, unlike my father, who barely spoke to his family. They met and married, and then he was gone serving on naval ships for much of their young married life. She stayed behind to raise two daughters. After my dad came home for good, he asked my sisters what they wanted more than anything, and they said a trip to Disneyland and a baby sister. That is where I came in.

I was born in 1960 into a turbulent nation that would weather life-changing events, such as the Cold War, the civil rights movement, and a presidential assassination that broke a nation's heart, along with the assassinations of much-beloved prominent men who had visions of a prosperous future America. We entered a war that most people felt was impossible to win. We would find ourselves in a fight to win the Cold War with a down-to-the-wire negotiation with Russia, all based on the fear of our nuclear stockpiles. We would grow by leaps and bounds when a president issued the challenge of sending a man to the moon before the decade was over. We could not stand to be second fiddle, and in spite of that, we did indeed place a man on the moon in 1969. I witnessed a transformation in the youth of the day very personally by having the quintessential hippie for a first cousin. She wore the beads, bell-bottom pants, long, straight hair with a headband, and a peace sign adorned her chest in several long strands of necklaces. She preached peace and brotherhood while experimenting with drugs that were known to be mind altering.

She even took a trip to New York, hitchhiking along the way to attend a then little-known song festival called Woodstock. Every time I visited her, I wanted to be her. She lived a life of freedom, with her own parents not even able to contain her hippie ways. Even to this day, in her sixties, she still gives off that hippie vibe I remember. I would have made a great hippie, minus the drugs. But I couldn't in my family.

My family consisted of a June Cleaver-type mom who stayed at home to raise three girls. Her job in the family was very well outlined, and she took it on with gusto. Every night, we ate a meal together that would take her hours to prepare from start to finish. Without speaking one note of disdain, we would dutifully attend church three times a week, twice on Sunday and once on Wednesday night. There was no reason good enough to miss church. You would have to be at death's door in the hospital on a ventilator not to be there, so I learned early on to just go with it. Thankfully, I thought it was fun, and I had many great friends there.

This strict evangelical doctrine shaped my young life in ways that would have me question whether I was going to heaven when I died. I was so scared that I was going to hell that I went out of my way to be good in all ways. I was the perfect child. I never got into that much trouble, because children were to honor their parents. It was in the Bible, and that was law that you did not mess with. I sat week after week through all my formative years being told that fire and brimstone awaited me if I did certain things, so, of course, I did not do those things. You might say this was a little extreme—and it was—but at that time, it was not out of the ordinary. Denominational churches were a dime a dozen and on every street corner. I also grew up thinking that everyone outside of my church was going to hell because they did not belong to "the church." Even at a young age, I had issues with this. I remember questioning the doctrine in Bible classes and getting in trouble when I got home because the teacher went and told my parents. As I got older, my questions grew, and I read and studied. If I read the Bible literally, then we were following exactly what it said, so I immersed myself in the doctrinal study of scripture.

Sunday night church was difficult for a young girl, because it was the night of the *Wonderful World of Disney* on TV. One perk of having to miss out on Sunday night Disney time—and this was before we could record the shows we missed—was that I could very easily get out of trouble using this very same religion to work for me. When I got in trouble once—and I cannot even remember what I did—I was sent to my room without supper. This was not acceptable to me, so I wrote the scripture, "Man cannot live by bread alone" and folded it up and slid it under my bedroom door. I could hear my sister pick it up and read it and take it to my mom, who promptly burst into laughter. This is how I learned to get my way and how to get out of trouble if I found myself in it. All I had to do was quote scripture to my mom, and it was like magic. It rendered her speechless, with proud laughter spilling from her, instead of her telling me how long I was grounded. I used it often, but not often enough for her to figure out it was a tactical move on my part. After all, I was just a kid, right? I would not be that manipulative, would I? Ask my husband that question and it becomes a different story. All of that made me memorize scripture. I had to memorize verses anyway for Bible classes, and this way, I just got a big perk out of it. To this day, I can quote verses verbatim, as many can do, I'm sure. The one good thing to come out of my limiting background was that I knew the Bible. I read it all the way through several times. I knew all the major characters and stories. I had a multitude of questions about all these stories as they were taught to me, but I dared not speak. It would not be until my brave teen years that I would challenge major doctrinal policies of my church with my Bible study leaders. I believe my spiritual transformation began at this point in my life when I studied so hard and had questions that my teachers could not answer.

Other than living by a strict standard set forth in the Bible, I had a somewhat normal childhood before the age of eight. I rode my bike everywhere. I had a pink banana bike with a straw basket on the handlebars. It was my main mode of transportation to get to my friends' houses, play in a nearby park, and chase boys who didn't want to be chased. We knew someone was home because there would be four or more bikes out front, so we would go in and visit. Many a time I stayed for supper at a friend's house. We played football in the yard and found a great place out in the field behind our houses where we could race each other on a circle of hills. It was great fun, and I remember it fondly. My parents never worried about me as long as I was home by supper on school nights and did my homework. I could be playing in a storm drain or getting a ride with a total stranger and they would never know. Back then, in the late 60s and early 70s, children did not have to worry about predators, or at least they didn't where I lived. There was no such thing as a computer or video games. Our form of play was riding our bikes and some TV watching. I was born with a black-and-white TV in my house, but shortly after that, our neighbors got a color TV. I remember seeing it for the first time with total amazement. I wonder if I will ever be able to fully explain to my grandchildren one day about how life was back then. They need to know, as it is a part of them, so I will give it a good try. I will most certainly read them a real book and not just one from an e-reader, even though I am a self-proclaimed e-reader addict.

Another great memory of my childhood was meeting and having two very best friends. I met my first best friend in elementary school, and we also went to church together. We fast became inseparable. We did everything together, as best friends do. There was not one weekend or vacation that we didn't spend together. I have lost touch with her over the years, which is a great regret of mine. It is one of those things that you say you are going to do something about and then never do. I met my next best friend in fifth grade. She moved to town and went to church with me. I met her when my other friend brought her to my house one day, and the rest, they say, is history. She just so happened to live on the same street as my other friend, and I lived one block over. That made it so easy to ride our bikes together and spend the nights together. We quickly became the three musketeers. We had great fun! There is not one memory I have of my elementary, middle, and high school days that does not have them in it. Being in the same church youth group also made it fun for all of us. I lost touch with them after I went to college. I went off to a different college, and that was that. I saw both of them when my mom was sick and at her funeral. It was like a day had not passed. We swore to stay in touch and exchanged phone numbers and e-mail addresses. I have e-mailed, but not as often as I would like. They are beautiful women with very different lives, as is mine. I wonder what they will think of this book.

I attended a public school system that was light years away from what it is today. Trying to make even the slightest comparison between the public schools of the 60s and 70s and today's schools is fruitless. I believe it is perhaps the greatest change in society and, at the same time, the most disappointing. The violence and lack of discipline, not to mention the disrespect shown to all members of authority, overshadows the stronger expectations we have of students today. Back in the day, we began each day with a prayer before the pledge. I believe this had a calming influence on everyone and allowed a tranquil start to the day. His holiness the Dalai Lama has said, "If every 8 year old in the world was taught to meditate, we would eliminate violence in the world within one generation." I wholeheartedly believe that meditation should be taught and practiced during the school day. I think it might help curb the growing violence that is prevalent in just about all public schools. I never disobeyed in school, and there was a good reason why. If I did, I got swatted with a ruler on my hands, or worse, my hair or ears were pulled, and it was painful. It was painful enough that I did not want it to happen again, because I knew my mom and dad would be waiting at home to give it to me again—but this time, with a belt. The whole corporal-punishment philosophy worked to curb behavior by scaring the daylights out of me, just like church did. It is a wonder I grew up without a death wish of some kind. Even through all of this—and there were scary times, like practicing for a nuclear threat—I thrived and grew up a "normal" kid. I believe every kid out there grows up with some level of difficult upbringing, and mine was no different—although the real horror was yet to begin.

CHAPTER TWO

Unspeakable

~◈~

It takes a strong person to forgive. The weak are not capable.
—Ghandi

This is the hardest chapter for me to get on paper. Nobody knew a word about what I went through for about eight years of my life. I kept this secret to myself for twelve years. The first person to hear this secret was my then future husband. It remained our secret for a dozen or so more years, until I learned that I was not the only victim. Years after learning this, I journaled my experiences, talked with a trusted mentor, and read countless books, all with one goal in mind: healing.

My mom was very close to her siblings. It just so happened that they were all sickly. Her two sisters in particular suffered from severe heart disease, even at early ages. Unfortunately, they were not blessed with loving families to care for them after they suffered a heart attack or were in the hospital, so my mom would pack up and leave for sometimes a few weeks at a time to take care of them. I never faulted her for this until it started happening.

We would have to have different people come in and help take care of us. My dad was gone a lot due to his long hours working as an air traffic controller. There was a lot to do with three young daughters, and at the time it began, none of us drove yet. It began with me when a close family member began to become too familiar with me. My hackles would rise, and I would feel very uncomfortable. This was my intuition warning me of danger, but I was only eight years old and did not realize it at the time. Nobody had given me the "stranger danger" talk or told me what to do if someone touched me in a private place. It was not done back then because it was so secretive, nobody knew it was such an issue. My innocent and trusting brain thought he was just being friendly. He started becoming increasingly brave and would touch me when nobody was looking. I would look around wondering if anyone saw, but nobody ever said anything. Then, one day, I was pulled "jokingly" into his lap. His hands started feeling around on me, and he even fondled my barely existent breasts. I pulled away, and he stopped. This only happened when he was "on call" to take care of us while Mom was away. I felt fairly safe as long as she was home, but then she began to be gone for longer periods of time, and my anxiety grew to epic proportions.

I found myself alone with this person a lot since my sisters were now of an age to be with friends. I tried to be away from my house by riding my bike as much as I could or at least walking up the street to friends' houses, but I had to come home eventually. Each time I came home, he would do the same thing. He would fondle me and feel me all over while he pulled me onto his lap. He swore me to secrecy, saying that my mom would not believe me anyway because I was just a kid. He scared me into remaining silent because I knew if I told, my mom's life would be forever changed. He also threatened my other sisters with the same treatment, so I kept my mouth shut. I learned to hide in my room with the door shut. He rarely came into my room, thank goodness, but when he did, the fear I felt was so crippling that to this day, there is no comparison. I could not speak or move. I felt totally alone. There was no one to talk to. The older I got and the more developed I became, the worse the abuse got. I used to hide my breasts behind big shirts whenever he was around. I would droop my shoulders to hide them and keep my head down and not look him in the eye. Why nobody ever noticed this is beyond me. It was so evident to me.

I learned the fine art of escapism by drowning myself in music. There is not a stronger case for the therapeutic effects of music than the way I utilized it. I listened to music from the time I got home from school until after I fell asleep. I would immerse myself in the lyrics and perform plays with perfume bottles being my microphone. I would devour books and television movies about strong, independent women that didn't put up with any bull and stuck up for themselves. I was convinced that this would inadvertently change the world. When I was old enough to realize that I was growing up a teenager right in the middle of the women's movement, I was so for that. It is easy to understand why. I wanted to join the National Organization for Women (NOW), but I was too young. It also went against my church's doctrine that women were to silently worship. They had no part in the service at all. That never resonated with me. Why did God make females, then? To just sit still and do what men told us? To produce babies? That just could not be true. My whole life, I have believed in the relentless power women possess. Through the process of waking up to my spiritual purpose, I have extended my belief to include the power inside each of us. I believe that if everyone owned his or her power, the world would be a very different place.

During those years of abuse, I learned to pray for safety when I was there alone and I knew he was in the other room. I would literally wait to go to the bathroom to pee or bathe until after I knew he was gone. I guess it helped when I became a teacher, because I could really hold it in well. Little did my fellow teachers know the reason behind my superior bladder control.

I remember the last time the abuse happened. I was sixteen years old and driving, and he started in with his normal routine. He would often suggest taking a shower together because he knew people who did that, so it was okay. Like I believed that. I was not a moron. So I just blurted out, "You are sick. You have a real mental problem, and it requires help. I will help you find a doctor to see, and I will make sure you get the help you need." Everything suddenly stopped. I guess I hit a nerve. He never asked me for help or touched me again. I was still scared it would not last, but I was getting older, and when I graduated high school, I was out of that town and headed to college.

What is the blessing in abuse of any kind? Are there lessons to be learned? I found the blessing to be the ability to help others in similar situations cope and learn the truth about their abuser and them, the victim. At this point, I want to say beyond a reasonable doubt that I should have told someone. Maybe not my mom, but my sisters, my teachers, or anyone else I felt close enough to confide in. I did not trust men at all at this point. I still liked boys, but never too seriously. I thought men would side with each other against me. It is extremely important for victims to know that they are not at fault. They are the unwilling victims of sick individuals. Many people out there are sick and will lash out in some abusive way to exert control they probably feel they do not have in other aspects of their lives. They might act out some sick compulsion or obsession they have that is unhealthy. I know you have heard that once a person is mentally ill in this way, they never get better, especially pedophiles. We have to approach it as that being the truth of the matter, so feeling like you can save that person is not reasonable or plausible. Getting away from the situation is key, and then finding a way to stay away or have that person removed from your world is the perfect scenario. Each case is different and needs to be handled individually because there are too many variables in each family. Evidently, talking to the person about his illness worked for me. I guess he just never had anyone call him out on it or verbalize it. Don't take the threats. That empowers them even more, and make no mistake, abuse is a power game. Don't give up your power to the person who is abusing you. Take it back!

How did I heal? Well, it took a large part of my adult life, and it was gradual, requiring hard work on my part and a lot of help on God's part. A turning point in my recovery came when I met the person who would become my spiritual mentor, Linda Drake. She had written a book about healing called *The Secret Pathway to Healing*. I devoured it. It came with a workbook type of journal where I recounted my experiences in detail, including the behaviors that resulted from the extreme emotions I felt. Then I analyzed those same types of behaviors that I saw in myself as an adult. There were many "aha" moments for me. The escapist behaviors were exactly the same type of escapist behaviors I used when I was being abused. I still escaped into my bedroom, listened to music therapeutically, and read voraciously. I slowly began to come out of my room and notice the times I felt the need to escape. As time passed, the need for escape to safety lessened and morphed into a way to give myself some much needed space from the demands of the day.

Another life-changing lesson was when I learned the vast importance of forgiveness. Many times, it is not just another person but also you who needs to be forgiven. That is even sometimes harder but is a key to getting on with life. Anger is such a big part of abuse, but forgiveness can be found on the flip side of anger. I began the process of writing down how I felt while the abuse was taking place. It was not easy to think about this, let alone write about it, but it was helpful. Writing is a proven form of healing that I found to be just what I needed. I put a name to each and every emotion and how that same emotion played out in my life today. I realized that the abuse was a crucial reason I was antisocial. I stayed holed up in my world of safety that I created. I only became social when I was out of my house. I was very social at parties, at work, and with friends, but the minute I came home, I headed to my safe bedroom. As soon as I realized it, I was able to change the behavior and the self-talk to statements of safety. The actual act of forgiveness was harder. It became easier overnight when I learned perhaps the most profound lesson I would ever learn.

Every person on earth is navigating his or her own personal journey, and there are lessons to be learned from daily life and significant life events. The lesson I learned was that abusers are on their own journeys as well. They have lessons to learn and, more importantly, maybe even to help you learn. This helped me to forgive when I understood that I was not responsible for his actions, only for the way I reacted. It was even suggested to me that some people come into our lives to sacrifice themselves to help us learn our lessons. Those people actually love in the most profound and proactive way. They no longer want to see you be a victim, so they seek to help you get past the victimization you feel in this lifetime. Whether or not you believe this, it does make it easier to forgive. Once I took a step back and separated the victim from the abuser, it shed a new perspective. I worked on removing all emotion from the situation and tried to view it as just another lesson that I for sure did not want to repeat. I learned that the way out of the karma was to forgive. Forgiveness is a process, but it can be done, no matter what the emotions are behind the experience. I found so many books that addressed the subject of forgiveness and read everything I could on the topic. I applied many suggestions, but one that stuck out as helpful to me was to gauge my reaction whenever I was around that person. Luckily, I was not around the person very often, but when I was, I went inside myself and tested my emotional waters. Did I feel anger, hatred, or pity? I went through the spectrum of emotions for a while, but then I gradually felt nothing. I regarded this as a true validation of my healing efforts through forgiveness. I believe forgiveness is essential to happiness, whether it be forgiving an abuser, a neglectful parent, or even yourself. Many people might question how I could ever forgive a family member for such unspeakable acts, but I think I have through hard work and intense self-reflection. I might have forgiven, but the healing is a whole other story.

If you are a victim of abuse right now, stop and make a conscious decision to work toward removing yourself from the situation. It could be that your lesson to learn is how to let go.

I once thought that healing was finite. There was a beginning and an end. It was a trip with a destination. Now, I am convinced that it is like an onion. It has many layers that are peeled back one at a time. After a layer is peeled, a sense of accomplishment is felt until the next layer rears its ugly head. I now feel like it is a lifelong process with periods of significant progress, so much so that the experience no longer has power. I learned this one fateful day when visiting with Linda, my mentor. She informed me that I had many other layers to peel back and they all involved my inner child. What? *What is an inner child?* I thought. Deeply embedded in our psyche is the still small child we once were. Everything that happened to us as children is still part of us in our soul's memory. This inner child needs to be healed too. Linda told me to remember back to the things that brought me joy as a child and pick a few to do. Well, that was not so bad. I loved to color, so when I made scrapbooks and cards, I could do that. I loved to watch movies from the 60s, and that would be fun too. The point was to make my inner child feel safe in this new world without the crippling fear she lived with for so long. I talked to her and tried to make her feel safe once again. In my studies, I came across a few really helpful strategies for helping heal the inner child.

Sandra Taylor is one of my favorite experts. I took her online course, The Ultimate Magnetic Power Intensive. It is one of the most valuable trainings I have ever done. Her philosophy is that our memories and reactions from our childhood can become encoded, and they need to be released. One aspect of her course is releasing and rescripting those negative experiences. Remember that energy can be changed, so you can write another ending to that memory. It is an interesting concept. Another expert, Carol Tuttle, says that she starts each new client out with a visualization exercise addressing the inner child. Her philosophy is that many feelings, emotions, and even physical pain can be tied back to the inner child. The scripts she uses makes the inner child feel safe and secure. It is well worth it to keep this in mind as part of the healing process.

I also learned something that, quite frankly, relieved me. I did not have to confront the person in order to heal from the situation. I never even have to see or speak to that person again in order to heal. Remember, healing takes place in the soul and subconscious, not by a face-to-face confrontation that ends in hugging and forgiving. In fact, chances are that would never happen anyway, so you are setting yourself up for failure if that is your expectation.

Remember that scene in *The Wizard of Oz* when Glenda the good witch tells Dorothy, "You had the power all along, my dear?"

Truer words have never been spoken. You are responsible for your own power. This realization made me feel, well, powerful. It was kind of like thinking, *You can't hurt me anymore, because I won't let you.* It is a self-assertiveness that is healthy and integral to healing from abuse of any kind. You are a child of God, and a child of God never deserves to be treated with anything other than honor and respect. If it does not honor you, get rid of it. I have a real problem with people who use their childhood abuse as an excuse for criminal behavior. The statistics on the amount of people who were and are abused as children are jaw-dropping. You don't see all of them crying in a packed courtroom for leniency because they had a bad childhood. In reality, probably all of us at some point can think of certain things in their childhood that made it bad. If you cannot, then consider yourself among the lucky ones who did not have that as a soul lesson here on earth at this particular time. The main point is that you have the power.

As an adult, you alone are responsible for the life you have now. You have the power to change it. You can heal, and it might even be your reason for being on earth now. Do whatever it takes to make this change happen, because it will be worth it. It certainly has been worth it to me. When you realize it is not your journey or your fault, that is a start. As I grew more in my spiritual journey, it became much easier to forgive others. I grew to know that we are such a small part of something much bigger than ourselves. We are on a journey to grow and learn, and forgiveness is a major part of this. When I could separate myself from the abuser and the situation and see it as a learning experience, removing all emotion, I could forgive. This takes time and going inside yourself and seeing yourself as one with God.

The important thing is to begin. Take those first steps toward your own path of healing. My first step was talking to someone else and writing down my experiences and feelings. This book is a healing experience for me as I write it. You might not agree and think that it is a waste of time, and my answer to that would be: give it a try. You will have awesome "aha" moments, I promise. You will find patterns and connections that explain why you are the way you are today and how you can change for the better. If you are in a deep depression or have fallen victim to addiction in any form, this is vital for your future well-being. Just pick up a pencil or phone. You owe it to yourself. Your purpose on this earth is to be happy. It is your birthright as a child of God.

CHAPTER THREE

What Do You Mean, No Dancing?

*Never be ashamed of a scar. It simply means you
were stronger than whatever tried to hurt you.*
—Buddha

My teen years could have led me to a life of addiction, crime, or some emotional breakdown, given my history. Instead, I loved my teen years and had many wonderful experiences that I now know were my first efforts at healing my trauma. I thank every single person who loved me and made my life easier. I knew I had a secret, but I immersed myself in friends and my church youth group, and they literally saved my life.

I was a natural-born dancer, in my own mind. I may not have been that good, but I had rhythm, and I loved it. I felt the music as music became my escape from the abuse. Even now, I can rely on music to take me away. I even found it cathartic to establish a list of the ten songs that make up the soundtrack of my life at this point. It was great fun to do and self-revealing as well. If you want to know how you are feeling, listen to the words of the music you like. I put on my 70s rock and I can clean house in record time, and workouts are much more enjoyable—when they happen. I am not exaggerating when I say that music saved me from myself. I dreamed of dancing like Elvis and his girlfriends in his movies. I even practiced, like any teenage girl in the 70s, by singing into my hairbrush in front of a mirror and dancing like there was no tomorrow. So when I learned that my church didn't allow dancing because they felt it was too suggestive and encouraged fornication, I was devastated. Being the good Christian girl, I did not question it, because it was God's will and the church said so. I just continued to dance away in my room all by myself, mourning the loss of cotillions and proms.

Don't get me wrong. I loved my teen years in my youth group at church. My best friends and I were leaders in the group. We were top dogs, and we loved every minute of it. We were all tagged with the label of being "goody two shoes" at school, but we didn't mind. We carried it like a banner on top of our pedestal that could never shake because we would not let it. No "wild oats" for us. We never tried smoking or drugs. I must admit that I did once willingly try whiskey, but it made me sick. That was the end of that less-than-wild oat. About the only other oat I ever sowed was a mild instead of a wild one. I willingly let a hunk of a guy get to second base in the backseat of his royal-blue Camaro. The definition of irony is that we had tried to "park" on the dead-end street not far from his house, but a neighbor came out with a gun, and we got out of there as fast as we could. So instead, we "parked" under the eaves of the local Church of Christ. Get the irony yet? It was hidden from the major road on the back of the property, and I was sixteen, so my hormones did not acknowledge it at the time. All I knew was that I would memorize the soundtrack of Boston's "Let Me Take You Home Tonight" and look back on it fondly for the rest of my life. It was definitely something I could see myself doing again, but good church girls don't do that, right? I was not to learn what second base was until later in life. I knew there were bases and they didn't have anything to do with baseball, but that was as much as I knew. I even tried to ask my mom once, but she never answered my questions. She would always take it back to the Bible, oddly enough. I once asked her why everyone talked about "making love." What was that? Kissing? Her answer just left me with more questions. So, I knew better than to bring up the *s*-word. See, I could not even say *sex* back then.

My mom never had "the talk" with me and didn't even warn me about my period. I learned about periods in school, but I guess I didn't pay good enough attention amidst all the snickers and snares. So when I started my period, I thought I was dying and was supremely insulted when I found out it was monthly. You are kidding me; how was I going to ride my bike?

My friends and I dated, but boys never got anywhere. Mostly, they were from our church, so that explains a lot. Except for the hunk that got to second base. I wonder if he ever had any idea that my time spent with him was so pivotal? I haven't seen him since high school, but if I ever do, I am still not saying a word.

My friends and I never debated church doctrine. We just had fun praising God and having set boundaries for our behavior that we never questioned. When I think about it, though, it is a good thing we never did question it, because it would have been considered blasphemous. I see the blessings in my teen years at church, and I am profoundly grateful. I learned the Bible inside and out and had very dear friends. It kept me safe and gave me my steadfast, deep, abiding love for God. That doesn't stop just because you abandon or question a doctrine. It is a birthright to be a child of God, no matter what the circumstances. I would learn this later on, but it is a cornerstone of my belief system now.

Fun was not only to be had from the youth group at church. My family, including my sisters, Mom, and I, had an obsession with all things Elvis. We loved his music and watched all his movies. As a family, each time a new movie came out, we would head out to the nearest drive-in theater. It is a shame they aren't around anymore. They were great fun. One weekend, we heard that Elvis was going to be in concert about two hours away, so we bought tickets. We packed up and left to spend the night with a family friend that lived not far from the venue. We were actually going to see him in person. I was only fourteen years old, but I had it just as bad for him as every other red-blooded American girl (or woman). Along with my best friend, my sister, my mom, and a family friend, we all went to see the legend in action. We each had our own pair of binoculars. I will never forget that opening music and my heart pounding as he took the stage. Sometime during the concert, he asked for the house lights to go up so he could take a good look at us. You could hear a collective gasp as every female in the audience moved to straighten her hair. At one point, women were charging to the stage. This was before the time of security not letting you get anywhere near concert performers. I took off from my seat, not asking anyone's permission or waiting for their comments. I approached as close as I could get in the crowd, when all of a sudden, I saw a scarf flying through the air. I jumped for it but missed. A nice man caught it, smiled big at me and handed it right to me. That man will never know the role he played in my life. What a memory! To paraphrase Sheldon Cooper, I now "possessed Elvis's DNA," because he wiped his sweat on it before he threw it. I would later learn that the guys who helped him on the stage threw out random scarves too, but I decided to believe I had one with his sweat on it. It had a cherished place in my room, and to this day, it is in a hidden place known only to me.

The day he died was sad for all of us. He was such a talent. Even now, my sisters and I will get together and have an Elvis marathon and watch his movies. They even took me to a theater for my fiftieth birthday to see a digital remake of one of his concert movies. I cried, not only because I was fifty but also because the memories overpowered me. In the car on the way home, I texted my son, who was in college at the time, and told him about how emotional I was and that I simply couldn't believe I was fifty. He texted back and said for me to remember that fifty is the new thirty. I simply texted back and asked him if that meant that twenty was the new two. Good times.

One of the highlights of my life was attending church camp every summer for four years. I loved it because I got away from home for two weeks to be with my friends. When I say church camp, I mean it in the strictest sense of the word. The boys were kept far away from the girls except at Bible study, chow, and evening social hour. The counselors would literally pull you away if you got to close to a boy. Once, I fell onto a boy's lap by accident and was promptly pulled off by a counselor as she whispered in my ear, "You are going to arouse him. Get up." After getting up and being supremely embarrassed, I wondered what *arouse* meant.

Our camps were in mid-summer and usually about 100 degrees in the shade. There was no air-conditioning anywhere except in the nurse's office. Needless to say, we all took sick at least once during camp. Sounds drab and dull and not fun at all, right? I loved it! I loved being with my girlfriends, washing our hair in the river, and the intense Bible studies that made me feel such a kinship to God that it is hard to duplicate to this day. The counselors might have been a little overbearing, but they wanted us to have fun. They arranged great concerts, social hours, and talent shows that were hilariously funny and wildly entertaining. I met a few boyfriends there and stayed in contact with some of them for years, even after camp was over.

One of the highlights of my time at camp came in my final year when I won one of the Campers of the Year awards. I had never won anything previously and this was an award that was voted on by the campers, so I was thrilled.

It's funny what you choose to remember from your childhood. The first thing I think about when I think of my camp days is the closing ritual every night before bedtime. We would get in circles holding hands out in a big field by the river with only the stars and moon shining singing every single verse of the song "My God and I." I get goose bumps every time I think about it.

Social religion had its place in society, and as a child from that era, it significantly helped to shape who I am today. When I think of all the trouble that was just waiting out there for me to get into, it is then that I thank my mom and God for blessing me with my church youth group. Finding solace in church or group activities can be very soothing. Friends or family members you can trust can be lifelines of support. As a teen, I did not have a whole lot of choices, so thank goodness I had the much-needed distractions that I did. I know that God put them there. So if you are going through a rough patch and you think God is nowhere to be found, it could be he is right there taking care of you, and you will realize it later.

You could even find out that he actually was arranging for future events that would take you out of the misery. I believe that God knows a whole lot better what is in our best interest than we do, and we just have to trust in that. The important thing is to never give up. The old saying, "This too shall pass," is a wise saying that rings true. You only need to hang on until you make it to the other side. If you need to, take it one day at a time, and celebrate the days as you get through them. At one point in my life, I was taking it hour by hour, but I made it through. Considering where I am now on my spiritual journey, I often wondered, *Why did God put me in such a strict church upbringing? Why did he make the rules so rigid?* Now I know why. Thank you, God.

CHAPTER FOUR

Is There Such a Thing as Love at First Sight?

⟨∞⟩

Whatever our souls are made of, his and mine are the same.
—Emily Bronte

There are seasons in every life, and the door that closes on one season always opens to another. I graduated from high school in 1978. I wondered why it was such a big deal. I was going to college. I was still going to be in school, but my family was so proud of me. Whatever; I was just looking forward to another era. I lived at home when I attended the local junior college for one year to help with expenses, but my real dream was to finish at a state university a few hours away. I even took a job as an aide to a calculus professor during that time to make a little money. You would have to know me personally to appreciate the irony, since I was not a math person. It ended up being okay because all I did was grade papers and type his doctoral dissertation.

Shortly before Christmas during my freshman year of college, my sister talked me into helping her run a "Santa and me" photo booth at the local mall. I had to dress like a lumberjack and be one of Santa's forest helpers while taking pictures of children on Santa's lap. It seemed like fun until I saw myself in my costume. I had jeans rolled up to my knees and a red flannel shirt with socks.

I had a toboggan on my head and felt I really must've looked like a real lumberjack, minus the muscles. Other young girls helped out too. One, in particular, I did not like. I may have grown up innocent, but I knew a slut when I saw one. All she did was flirt with all the dads and brothers and complain about the kids. I just ignored her and did my job.

One day, as we were finishing, this very handsome policeman came up to me and asked me if I was the girl he was talking to earlier. I threw up my hands and said no, thinking that she had worked her magic on yet another unsuspecting male and he was out of luck because she was gone. He abruptly changed his tune very apologetically and said he just got us confused and thought we might need a policeman to walk with us to the car since we were carrying cash. I thought, well, if he didn't recognize her, then maybe he was telling the truth. I relaxed and said, "Sure, why not?"

We finished closing down the shop, but the entire time, he stared at me. I felt an odd feeling that was both flattering and brand new for me. It was kind of like what you read about in romance novels. My stomach did a flip-flop, and I immediately became aware of how I must've looked. He walked my sister and me to the car, spending a little extra time walking beside me. I couldn't help but notice he had honey-colored hair and a cute smile. He looked pretty alpha in his police uniform, but I never thought he would be interested in me. He was a man, and I was just a kid right out of high school. I learned that he was an off-duty cop working overtime at the mall for extra money. I lay in bed that night wondering what it would be like to date a cop.

The next day during a class, I told my good friend about the new guy I had met, but I didn't even know his name. I had gotten a glimpse of his nametag, but all I saw was a *G*. I described him, and she said that I had met Grant Critchfield. She happened to know him and gave me a brief history of going to the same high school. He was apparently a football hotshot who'd made a lot of touchdowns. He was also quite popular, class president, and quite a catch. Wow! That gave me something to think about.

After class, I went home to get ready for work at the mall. As soon as I walked through the door, my sister and my mom were sitting at the kitchen table staring a hole through me. "What?" I asked. My sister replied, "That cop came by today looking for you. He is coming back tonight to see you."

I couldn't believe it. I ran into the bathroom, showered and washed my hair with extra conditioner, and did a top-notch job of shaving. I rolled my hair and sat under the hair dryer, and yes, I had one with a cap on it. I must admit, I didn't look half bad after spending two hours on hair and makeup. However, I still had to wear the lumberjack outfit. Ugh!

When I got to the mall, he was already there. He was out of uniform and off duty, so he came by early. I told him my shift was four hours, but he chose to wait on me. He made me nervous just standing there seemingly staring at me. Every time I glanced his way, he was already looking at me. I just focused on the kids—or tried to. After I finished working, he asked me out on a date. I kept thinking to myself, *I wonder if he waited around this whole time just to ask me out.*

The big day approached, which was a Wednesday, but I had church. Of course I never missed church, so we had to go out after that. I became increasingly excited. My sisters and Mom were no help at all.

Finally, the doorbell rang. We went to a local pizza place, and when we left, he said, "You want to go to my place?" I then wondered if he had his own place. Wow. How old was he? I was only 18. He didn't look that much older. The word *yes* came out of my mouth before even thinking about it. I remember thinking, *What have I just done?* I knew he wasn't a bad guy, so I decided to trust my judgment.

He lived in a one-bedroom efficiency apartment while serving as the apartment's security. It was a cost-saving move on his part, so his rent was free.

He turned on the TV, but it had been a hand-me-down from his grandmother, and we could only see the top half of the screen. Clearly, it was very old and did not work properly. Instead of watching Johnny Carson, we decided to listen to records. Yes, records, the vinyl kind. I chose to listen to Debby Boone's "You Light up My Life." While it was playing, he came and sat next to me on the couch. You know that song "This Magic Moment?" Well, that is exactly how I felt the first time he kissed me. It was literally like fireworks going off. He felt it too. There was no turning back for me; I was already a goner. I went to bed that night wondering what it would be like to be married to a cop.

After that day, we were inseparable. Not one day went by for years that we did not see each other. I was smitten from the beginning, and so was he. There was a euphoria going on between us that I am sure could not even be duplicated with drugs. Part of this good Christian girl just kind of morphed into a one-track-minded girl in love.

We spent all our time together at his apartment. I would search the newspapers for movie titles so I could tell my mom what the movie was about that we did not go to. We made up all kinds of things to tell my mom. I don't know if she ever caught on, but I never asked, not even as an adult.

One day, it kind of came out that he was planning on going back to college. He had been in college but ran out of money. He had become a policeman to save up and return to school at some point. As it turned out, it was the same college I was going to in the fall. Coincidence, anyone? We were both planning on leaving at the same time and never even knew it. I love the old saying, "Coincidence is just God's way of remaining anonymous." Yep.

We ended up living in the same apartment complex, because back then, you just didn't live with each other before marriage; or at least, in our world, you didn't. We spent all our time together, even in spite of tens of thousands of other girls and guys around us.

We decided to get married my junior year. The only problem that I had not addressed fully in my mind was the fact that, at my church, he was not considered "Christian" or "saved." This did not sit well with him. His church was way at the other end of the spectrum. Our doctrines could not have been any more different. Mine was ultra-conservative and his, not so much. I wanted so badly for him to conform, but that was just not in his nature. Grant would attend services with me but was clearly not welcomed. When we went to collaborate with church leaders, my preacher very brazenly and unapologetically told my future husband that he was going to hell because he did not belong to "the church."

That pretty much did it for him. I was pretty mad too, but after twenty years of church brainwashing, I was at a loss as to what to do. I wanted to continue going to that church, but I would have to go without him. I even tried to appease Grant by going to church with him occasionally. It was so different from mine. My mind would not stop with all the doomsday "fire and brimstone" scenarios. We would never resolve this issue until our children would make the decision for us much later. It bothered me so much that I got physically sick the spring before the wedding. I contracted mononucleosis, and as a complication, I developed a heart condition associated with the Coxsackie virus.

I had to drop out of college that semester due to hospital stays and surviving the illness itself. The recuperation was long and difficult. Each time I healed from one virus, I would get another. It was unlike anything I had ever heard of, and the doctors even had a hard time with their diagnosis. Looking back, I see now that my emotional state had morphed into the physical when I got sick, and it wasn't just a coincidence that it was a heart condition. I lost a ton of weight and had a rough time of it, but we kept the wedding date the following August. We decided to marry outside of the church because I wanted instrumental music and my church would not allow instruments. We married in the garden behind Grant's parents' home on a beautiful, tree-lined creek. We even had an organ moved outside so we could have some wedding music. It was mid-August and 100 degrees in central Texas.

I remember wondering right after taking our vows if we were both going to hell now. Not every bride can say that is what she thought after reciting wedding vows, but there it was, staring me in the face. Had I just made the biggest mistake of my life? Here I was breaking the rules by marrying an "outsider." I was going to hell by proxy, by osmosis.

I look back on those hard days of fighting with my inner self while at the same time loving him so much that I convinced myself none of it mattered. I was waking up in a very dramatic way to my own spiritual journey. What a wake-up call. I'd rather wake up to a bone-shattering alarm clock.

We would both graduate from college and settle into married life, but we still never really addressed the elephant in the room. Years later, our two young children attended a local summer vacation Bible school at a different church. They came home and excitedly said they wanted that church to be our new church. It just so happened to be doctrinally about halfway between our two belief systems. We also met some wonderful people who would grow to become good friends. Out of the mouths of babes and just like that, we had a new church home that would take our kids through high school.

You know that Garth Brooks song called "Unanswered Prayers"? Well, it really resonates with me because if I had married a preacher like I had wanted all of my younger years, I would not be where I am now. After being married thirty-five years with two great, successful, and independent kids, I can do nothing but thank my husband with all of my heart that he caused me to think about my whole religious belief system. Did I really think he was going to hell? Was I too, since I married him? I truly entertained the thought back then, but I've grown so much since that time. It is one of those "if I knew then what I know now" scenarios, because it all seems to be a ridiculous idea now. It did bother me that others thought this, including possibly my own parents, although they loved Grant. I know now that we were meant to be. There is no other plausible reason for us to have met, especially the way we did. We instantly felt like we had known each other all our lives. We were so comfortable with each other. We both believe we were destined to meet and marry to get us to where we are today in our souls' journeys. We have helped each other shape a belief system that we finally feel is our "home."

Even through all the heartache I went through and all the years struggling to find a church home, I can say it was worth it. I am very happy and comfortable today in my spiritual journey. I think a lot of people are rewriting their beliefs and realizing the difference between religion and spirituality. All I can say is you develop your own truth as you educate yourself and experience things that have the potential to change your current belief system. As Deepak Chopra so eloquently said, "Religion is belief in someone else's experience. Spirituality is having your own experience." The way I know I am living my own truth is that I feel like I am home. That is the best way I know to put it. Everyone has his own truth on his journey, and if it is your truth, it is not wrong. Honor it, but be tolerant of others and their journey, and as you become more mature in your belief, remember it is okay to change it. It could even be considered the growth of the soul.

CHAPTER FIVE

The Day My Faith Died

❧

Tears are prayers too. They travel to God when we cannot speak.
—Psalms 56:8

Life is not easy. Some even say that hell is here on earth. I don't quite know how my personal truth fits into that, but I do know that life will hand you moments that you will find so difficult to bear, you will question the very faith you grew up believing in with all your heart. Such a thing happened to my husband and me. After several months of trying to get pregnant without luck, we went to a fertility doctor. We both underwent tests, and it was determined that I was not ovulating and needed a fertility drug to induce ovulation. We were excited because we were starting to think we could not have children. It took four months for these drugs to finally work and for me to get pregnant. The day we found out was the happiest day of my life, bar none.

I had wanted a baby for so long. We had been married four years and were each established in jobs, and we were just ready. We were on cloud nine the entire time I was pregnant. I was treated like a queen by everyone. My husband would read and talk to the baby in the womb, which I found incredibly cute. I read books and prepared a nursery, even making my own curtains.

At about twenty-seven weeks, one day, I woke up with a backache. I just did not feel well at all. I called the doctor and he said not to worry but if it got worse to call him back. He was really busy that day and could not see me right away.

I waited and rested throughout the day, but I felt so different. Then I passed a bit of blood and really started worrying. I called the doctor again and he told us to meet him at the ER as soon as we could get there. We went right away, but by the time I was seen, I had started having contractions.

I learned later that I had passed the mucous plug and that meant the baby might come early. They decided to give me drugs to stop the contractions and also drugs to develop the baby's lungs just in case the contractions could not be stopped. The doctor told my husband to keep a log of the contractions noting the time and duration. I could not take anything for the pain because it would counteract the medicine to stop the contractions, so I endured contractions for fifty-four hours. They were logged as coming every one to three minutes. I still have the paper towel he used to write down all the contractions with the time and duration of each one.

The medicine was clearly not stopping the contractions, so they increased the dosage to develop the baby's lungs. The goal now was just to keep the baby in as long as possible to give the lung medicine time to work. After about fifty-four hours, I felt the urgent need to push. I was fully dilated and could not hold it anymore. I pushed and gave birth right there in the room in a nanosecond. The baby was immediately taken to the neonatal nursery while I was taken to the delivery room to retrieve the placenta and repair any damage. I was elated, because I now had a baby girl.

I immediately wanted to know how to get my milk to come in so I could nurse. Each person who came in tried to prepare me for what might happen next. I see it now as I look back, but I was blinded at the time. I think it was God helping me to cope. They had to take the baby to another hospital that was better equipped to handle preemies. It was as they thought; the baby's lungs were not as developed as they should have been. The nurses gave me something to help me sleep because I was physically and emotionally exhausted. My husband and all the grandparents left to go with the baby. I was glad she was not alone, but I wanted so desperately to be with her. I did not even get a good look at her before they took her.

Just after midnight, they came in to tell me that my baby girl had died. What? It had never crossed my mind that she would die. God was taking care of her and had her in his care. He would never allow that to happen. It must be a mistake. But it was not a mistake.

The hours that followed were a blur. Endless family and friends came in to express their sympathy. My poor husband was left to handle the funeral details because they would not let me leave the hospital. I had some damage that required repairs and needed time to let them heal. He went with my brother-in-law to make the arrangements. The funeral would be the very next day. I truly believe my husband was trying to spare me by scheduling it so soon so maybe I could not be there. His heart was in the right place, but after talking with the doctors, they suggested that I be released to attend the funeral for my own personal well-being and some much-needed closure.

I agreed, but they would only let me go if I went to my mom's house for a few days to recuperate, since her house was a few minutes from the hospital and our house was fifteen miles away. I don't remember much about the funeral except that I was just in shock. I could not speak, and I could barely walk. I just existed. Since our spiritual practices were so different, we had two different pastors to speak at a graveside service with family only in attendance.

All I could think was that my daughter was in the ground. Was she cold? Of course not. What if it rained? Stupid ideas, right? Needless to say, my faith was tested big time. It was exactly one week before Christmas when we buried her, and I was supposed to celebrate the birthday of my Jesus in one week. My Jesus who took my baby. How was I supposed to do that? Impossible.

My mom was the perfect mother. She tended to me and gave me the treatments I needed to heal. We stayed until Christmas and then went home. My husband had cleaned out the nursery, because he again wanted to spare me. It was still hard. I just existed. Everything reminded me of her. I had stretch marks, but no baby. I had my milk come in, but no baby. I had gained a bunch of weight, but no baby.

Thankfully, help came in numerous ways. One of the best things I remember getting was a package in the mail from a friend, and it included the stages of grief and grief-counseling information. It also contained a list of names of other parents who'd had similar experiences to call or write to and numerous agencies that offered help in various ways. It was the first time I had heard about the stages of grief, and I would keep up with my stages for many months. People grieve in different ways. I don't think there is a right or wrong way to grieve, but there is a destructive and nondestructive way. My own mother could not understand my grieving process. She thought I was holding everything in and I needed to get it out. That may have been true, but this was my particular way of grieving at the time. There is also no time limit on grief.

In many ways, I still grieve for Sarah because I miss her and wonder what life would have been like had she lived. I think it is important to allow yourself time to grieve. It won't be okay overnight. Luckily, we had an overabundance of support from my church home and my husband's as well. The cards and memorials were nice, and I even got a very nice letter from the doctor that just so happened to be passing by my room when Sarah literally popped out. He was "chosen" to deliver the baby. I went through the anger stage at my obstetrician, who I thought should have seen me sooner to avoid a premature birth. We even wondered whether it was God helping us because she would have had lifelong medical problems and he was trying to spare us a life like that. None of that made much sense to me. I read books and articles, talked to pastors, counselors, friends, and family, and I still got no answers. I even read a book that was supposed to tell me why bad things happen to good people, but I came away with more questions than answers. This was not the God I knew or grew up honoring and respecting on a daily basis.

On the day I was to return to work teaching, I did not quite know how I was going to get through the day. The last time I was at school, one of my more troubled students told me he hoped something happened to my baby. How could I face this boy now? Would he be sorry he said that? Well, he wasn't sorry and even said he was right. Yes, some students are like that, and he was only nine years old but very troubled.

The straw that broke the camel's back was when a parent came in to ask me if a goody bag was all I was planning on giving my students for Christmas. I had made each of them a goody bag with an ornament I made myself and other candies and things like pencils and erasers. It was not cheap, as I had around thirty students. Her comment did it for me. Was I supposed to be her son's Santa? I walked out of my room, up to the principal's office, and resigned. I just was not ready to deal with that yet, and we would have to find a way to make it financially, but that did not even factor into my decision at that point. It was not just my students and that parent; it was also the fact that one of my fellow teachers was the daughter of the doctor who had, in my opinion, waited too long to see me that day. I was still so angry and could not face her. She knew but said nothing.

So who was this God that had allowed this unspeakable tragedy to happen? It would be many, many years before I ever got an answer that resonated with me. I went on to have other children, thankfully, and time does help. However, I can say without a doubt there is not a day that goes by that I do not think of my Sarah, and she would be thirty years old this year. I went back to teaching when a job opened up at a school in a nearby neighborhood. I loved the school and the students and stayed there until my recent retirement. I am glad I decided to give it another try and not base all of teaching solely on a bad year at a campus that just did not suit me at the time.

So what does one do with this type of tragedy? Are there blessings to be found? One blessing that came out of our shared experience was the closer relationship my husband and I naturally developed. We helped each other. No subject was off-limits. No theory unapproachable. It helped so much to have someone go through this with me, but it was still my journey. He had his own journey to get through. Another blessing was our ability to help others in a similar situation. A few years after Sarah died, a colleague of my husband lost her daughter in a similar fashion. He wrote her a long letter about out ordeal and how we coped and gave her some reading material that had been helpful to us. We got a sweet letter back and still get Christmas cards from them. They now have two beautiful children. I believe there are blessings to be found in every situation if you look hard enough for them and pay attention to the signs.

I came across a really good book by Betty Eadie called *Embraced by the Light,* and it changed my whole outlook on death and the afterlife. She had a near-death experience and went to heaven. Her beautiful way of describing her experiences there profoundly changed me and it helped, but I was still a long way from healing. My whole way of dealing was to blame myself. If I had taken better care of myself and not let myself get so tired, things would be different. If I had just gone to the hospital on my own, things would be different. You can literally go on and on with the blame game, but let me tell you, it only leads to more heartache, and you are no better off and still have no answers. I would go back and forth with this blame game for more than twenty years before I would meet a person who explained it to me in a way that resonated with me and made sense.

Remember, I grew up in an evangelical household. I had always thought about things like, *Why have I always been so scared of fire and bridges and water? Where did that come from? What do you mean, I won't recognize my loved ones in heaven?* I vividly remember the day I was told that in Bible class. That was an "aha" moment for me because there was no way I would ever believe that. These were all questions I had but could never ask them when I was younger. My truth was changing due to all of my life events, but this would change my thinking in the most profound and basic way.

I have a good friend and mentor to me on my journey of waking up. Her name is Linda Drake, and she has counseled me and helped me in numerous ways. One session with her is like ten years with a psychotherapist. She told me that Sarah was here to help me learn a lesson of love. My future children would benefit from my loss by having a loving and devoted mother. She chose to sacrifice herself to help me with this lesson. I wondered why I needed to learn that lesson. I plan on asking that one when I get back home to heaven. It was obviously set up in advance of her birth and mine. I strongly suspect it has something to do with another life and time. In fact, I think a lot of things we encounter are related to a previous incarnation. Her words made sense with what I had learned about each of us having our own journey, and sometimes, our journey is to help others with their journey.

I still had doubts because that was not what I was brought up to believe, but could it be that I died in a fire at some point back in time and now in this life, I cannot even light a match because I am and have always been too scared? Yes, that made sense to me. What about the unexplainable fear I have when driving across a bridge that has water underneath it. Did I drown at one point in another life? A lot of people suffer from irrational fears and phobias that are hard to explain. Even if I did not admit that I believed in what she said, I really did.

I began to get my faith back as I shifted my belief system. I began to believe in the concept of life lessons and how there is no such thing as a coincidence. Everything happens for a reason to teach us something that our soul needs to learn. I slowly regained my need for prayer. I had an overwhelming desire to forgive. I had to forgive myself, the doctors, the nurses, my husband, and everyone even remotely involved, especially God.

How did I forgive? Well, the undeniable fact is that life goes on whether we want it to or not. It even goes on whether we are active participants or not. This personal tragedy actually jump-started me back on my own personal journey of transformation spiritually. I now had a whole new set of questions to research. Time has also helped a great deal. I blamed myself and had to do a life's worth of introspection before I was able to forgive myself. I did not truly forgive myself until I learned that Sarah had been on her own short journey and her purpose was to help me. Wow! Talk about mind-blowing. I am convinced that this is true, but I also believe she had other things to do with her little short life, and I plan on asking her one day what those were. One way I thought would be therapeutic for my own self-forgiveness would be to make quilts for newborn babies in the neonatal unit. I love making them. I also looked into volunteering to rock babies who had nobody to rock them. My local hospital had stopped that practice but is going to reinstate it. I will be the first to sign up, and I will bring a quilt with me. I had a hard time with Mother's Day when a local pastor told me to focus on my mom and mother-in-law instead of my loss. It was good advice and has helped me through thirty Mother's Days.

I felt like deep down, I had grounds for bringing a lawsuit against the doctor who was too busy to see me even though my symptoms were shown to be early labor. I later learned that he had been up all night and was fatigued, and that might have factored into his decision to blow me off until I went into full labor. But then I realized that was his journey. He learned a valuable lesson. Hopefully, he never blew anyone else off or at the very least, placed them with another doctor if he could not do it. I forgave him and know that he probably struggled with his actions and the outcome. That is hell, in my book. Filing a lawsuit is not my style, so I never pursued it. If you believe in predestination, then no matter what the doctor did or what I did, it was destined to happen to fulfill her purpose. I believe in this because she had no free will. I believe free will plays a large role in our destiny here on earth and how it all plays out. She did not have that. Believe it or not, I was even mad at my husband. I was too tired having to work full time and deal with the troubled students in my classroom. It was very stressful. But when I saw the effect Sarah's death had on him and the way he took care of me after she died,

I forgot all of that. God was easy to forgive. I did blame him for a while, but the whole reason why bad things happen to good people has been answered. These experiences, good or bad, are given to us to grow and learn our life lessons. Our choice is how we deal with them. God is here to help us through them, thank goodness.

How do I help you if you are going through a similar ordeal? I tell you that it is not God's fault. I tell you that your soul has lessons in this life to learn. Some of these lessons come hard and fast. Some involve abandonment, abuse, health issues, grief, natural disasters, and even the death of a loved one. There is always something to take away from whichever of these happen to you. I think of it as my soul's development, kind of like a lesson in school you learn. You learn in order to advance to the next level; it's the same with your soul. Just know that you are never alone. Help is as near as simply asking for it. Remember, though, that just because you don't get an answer or the answer you were wanting doesn't mean the prayer has not been answered. You may never know what might have happened if your prayer had been granted the way you wanted. You might find out later and thank God that he did not give you what you wanted. The saying, "Be careful what you wish for" is very true. I have learned to be as specific as I possibly can in prayer. You know the old saying, "That which doesn't kill you, only makes you stronger?" I believe that with all of my heart. I am a much more compassionate, caring, and patient person given my life experiences. I realize the difference between a huge problem and a minor nuisance because it seems that just about everything pales in comparison to the tragic events that have unfolded in the various stages of my life.

Today, am I healed from this tragedy? Yes, in the respect that I have forgiven all involved, but the hardest to forgive was myself. I talk to Sarah a lot, and my grown son has claimed all his life that she is his guardian angel. Even as a small child, he thought this. Maybe that was part of her journey to help him through his life. I don't know any of this for sure, but it does provide comfort.

In closing, I must say I am not finished healing. I am not sure I will ever truly heal, because there is a hole in my heart that will never be filled. I am okay with that because it is what it is. I take my greatest comfort in knowing I will see her again and she is now up with my mom and other loved ones that have passed on. I don't believe for one moment what I was taught when I was little, that we will not recognize our loved ones when we die. We will, and they are they waiting for us, and they are helping us each day. They will be ready to escort us as we pass, and we will be overjoyed to see them again.

CHAPTER SIX

Miracles

~⚜~

I knew when I met you an adventure was going to happen.
—Winnie the Pooh

My husband and I never really knew if we would be able to get pregnant again. We wanted to, that was for sure. I got back on fertility drugs, and we just hoped for the best. Lo and behold, we ended up pregnant after only four months. We were so happy, but deep down, we were worried that the same thing would happen again. It clouded our happiness, but just a little. We learned that we were having a girl and set about doing what everyone does to get ready.

About six months into the pregnancy, I went into labor. We were so scared, but this time we knew the signs and thought we could stop it. I was put directly into the hospital. It is so easy to recall because as soon as I got into the room and turned on the TV, the space shuttle Challenger had just exploded. My heart rate accelerated, which was counter to the medicine to stop the labor, so they made us turn off the TV. The labor was stopped, but we lived too far from the hospital for the doctor's liking, so we went to live with my parents. If anybody has ever had to go back home after being gone for eight years between college and being married, it was difficult, to say the least.

My poor mother was a saint. She took my bad moods and frustration in stride and made life so easy for me. I never really fully thanked her, and for this I am truly sorry.

Behind the scenes, my husband carried the burden of an $800-a-month bill for my medicine. The medication to keep me from going into labor was relatively new and not covered by insurance. He purposely did not tell me because he knew I would worry, and that would be bad for the baby. Needless to say, the financial burden was great, but it was so worth it.

Trying to keep busy was the hardest thing. Lucky for me, I am crafty and had all kinds of things to do. One thing I am never is bored. Seven weeks later, at thirty-eight weeks, my water broke. I went in to tell Mom and told her I was going to have this baby by the time Days of Our Lives was on at noon. Talk about setting an intention! My husband was called, and we loaded towels into the car for me to sit on and went to have our baby. Thirty-eight weeks was more than enough time for the baby to be developed, we hoped. As it turned out, she was a healthy seven pound, seven ounce baby girl. Needless to say, Shelley Rebecca became our life! She was so spoiled, and the whole family, on both sides, doted upon her. I hope her husband forgives us because we created the monster and he now has to carry on the tradition of perpetuating the "princess syndrome," as I call it.

The lessons I learned while trying to patiently keep from going into labor were numerous. I learned to really pray. I had always been one to pray, but I always thought the prayers of the men at church were so eloquent. I wanted to use words that were not only effective and specific, but pretty too. I practiced and wrote down my prayers. I found the words just flowing out of me, and I would understand much later that spirit was helping me with my prayers. Also, while writing this, I snapped on the fact that I did, in fact, set an intention to have this baby within just a few hours of my water breaking. Well, the labor was just shy of four hours, and I wonder, did I manifest that by setting an intention? I believe so. I purposely set an intention each morning for the day including what I wish to accomplish. It is so easy to do and produces great results.

I also learned that money doesn't matter when you are talking about a baby's life. We made it through financially, but I am glad my husband didn't tell me.

Lastly, but most importantly, I learned that you should tell the people in your life every day that you love and appreciate them. The one thing I regret most, now that my mom has passed, is all the missed opportunities to thank her and tell her how much I loved her. Don't wait. Tomorrow is promised to no one.

When our princess was seven months old, she came within hours of death. I came home from work to pick her up at my mother-in-law's house. I was so lucky, because she did not see day care for the first three years of her life. My mom and mother-in-law took turns watching her. When I arrived to pick Shelley up, she was listless. She literally did not move. She was like a limp dishrag. My mother-in-law said she had been like that for a little while and was more than likely coming down with something. I decided to take her to the doctor simply because the behavior was so unlike her, even when she was sick. My intuition was working big time, and I paid attention.

After checking her out, the pediatrician on duty told us to take her home and wait it out to see if other symptoms developed. I came unglued! There was no way I was taking her home in that condition, so I called her regular pediatrician at home, and he came right away. Her condition was worsening, so she was put in the hospital. I held her the entire time in a rocking chair, watching as she listlessly drifted away from me. She began to vomit nonstop. The next day, they still had no diagnosis. I was beginning to get angry on top of my growing fear. Clearly, there was something very wrong. The doctors were doing all kinds of tests, but it wasn't fast enough. When my baby started to throw up her own bile, I lost it. I screamed until I was heard. Not an hour later, the doctors came and said they wanted to do a barium enema on her to take a look at her intestinal tract. A resident had begun thinking outside the box, did some research, and discovered a rare telescoping of the small intestine into the large intestine called an intussusception.

This test would prove the resident was correct. If it was positive, it would also mean that her life was in danger and immediate surgery would be needed. Shelley went in at midnight for the test. Our whole family was there, but Grant and I could not sit still. We paced the halls praying to God to please not let us lose another child. We simply could not bear it. About forty minutes later, our pediatrician came out and said Shelley was going to be taken to surgery right away. The diagnosis of the resident was spot-on. Thank God for her. I still can see her sweet face some twenty-eight years later. It was a matter of a fresh mind and eyes looking at an old problem that old ideas and eyes did not recognize.

Our baby girl made it through just fine, but we were told that she would not have lived to see morning. Talk about divine intervention! Oh, how we cherished that little girl, and we still do.

CHAPTER SEVEN

The Call

⚜

It is both a blessing and a curse to feel things so deeply.
—David Jones

When our princess was eighteen months old, I got the call. You know how you remember where you were when JFK was killed, or for the young ones, 9/11? Well, I will never forget this day. I received a phone call like that. My college roommate, Lori, who was one of my dearest friends, was missing. She had just disappeared!

She was an elementary school teacher in a town about three hours away, and she had a second job at the local mall. She got off work from her mall job and was never seen again. Her car was even nowhere to be found. I was numb! You hear about these things happening, but you never think it could happen to you or your loved ones.

I was so worried about her parents. What must they be going through? Then there were her brother and sister.

At my school, my principal and fellow teachers were so supportive. I posted her license plate number and vehicle description everywhere, but I knew deep down that there was something sinister about this.

Details slowly emerged, and each one was more troubling than the last. We learned that her home was broken into and there were signs of struggle. They found an earring on her carpet, and the cords to her blow dryer and curling iron were ripped off. We could only speculate what that meant. She obviously made it home, and the going thought was that she had interrupted a burglary.

They later found her car abandoned in a parking lot near her home, and there was blood in the trunk. This was before DNA testing, so hopes of finding the person became a chore for local police, who investigated the old-fashioned way.

In the town where she lived, her friends and family orchestrated a search. She was so genuine and selfless. Everyone loved her! We felt so helpless being three hours away, but our local news was all over the story since this was her hometown. We decided we would head out and help in the search that had been planned for the coming weekend. My husband and brother-in-law had the police background, so they knew what to expect. I, on the other hand, was scared that we would find something bad—really bad.

It was the first time we had ever left our new daughter alone. We left her for the weekend with a very content grandmother who thought the sun and moon set with her precious granddaughter. She was in good hands.

It was strange that on the drive there, the radio played a Kenny Rogers tribute. I remembered he was Lori's favorite performer. I recalled a funny story that happened when we were in college. We went to a Kenny Rogers concert at Six Flags. She knew the seats were first come, first served, and she wanted a good seat, so she got there four hours early. We thought this was ridiculous, but there was no talking her out of it. She proudly sat on the first row chatting with band members and generally having a great time while waiting. She even sat beside Kenny's mother during the concert! They talked and talked. It was truly an awesome moment for her. When the rest of our crowd arrived, we finally understood, because our seats were in the nosebleed section while she happily sat beside Kenny Roger's mother in the front row listening to stories about his childhood. I always wanted to someway let Kenny know of his influence on my friend, but I never did.

We drove for three hours early that Saturday morning and met search crews at the local church where she attended. The mood was so somber, and her parents looked so tired and lost. I felt so bad for them, but at least I was doing something, finally. The search was conducted all over the city with groups of ten or so taking different areas. We spread out our arms and walked virtually fingertip to fingertip through a field on the outskirts of town. It was clear by this point that we were searching for a body.

It had been several weeks since she had gone missing, and a man had been arrested but was not talking. Our search only yielded a dead dog, and that was traumatic enough for me. No search teams found anything. We went home at the end of the day, but others planned to broaden the search to include area lakes and landfills. That piece of information alone broke my heart.

It seemed each piece of news like that was worse than the last. Three days after we got home, I was at school and I was called to the principal's office. This was unusual but not uncalled for. Naturally, I thought I was in trouble. Jeez, what was I, nine years old? When I got to his office, my mom and sister were there. I knew immediately that they had found Lori. I could tell by the look on their faces that it was not good. My principal told me to sit down, and I just burst out in a cry that I felt so deeply that it was overpowering. It was like it was coming from a place inside me that I never knew existed. A good friend of Lori's had not given up searching and went out on his own on some private property. He found her in a shallow grave wrapped in a plastic garbage bag, naked and with gunshot wounds to her head.

The world shifted, and the slow-motion thing began again. It was all over the news, as her funeral was planned for my town, where she had grown up. My husband was a pallbearer, and I was okay with this, but I needed him so badly by my side. He was my rock. My family sat behind the family section, with my dad escorting me. My husband would be with me in a few minutes. I just had to hang on until then. Her funeral was attended by more than five hundred people, with standing room only in the church where we both grew up. The man they had arrested was charged and convicted of capital murder and sentenced to death row. He would die of AIDS several years later in prison.

How does one find any blessings in such a tragedy as this? Well, I didn't for a long time. I went through the normal grieving process and had questions that were never answered. Years later, I could never shake the thought that she was with me. I would think of her all the time. Little things would happen when I thought of her. Once, I actually saw a ball of light dancing on the blinds covering my window while getting ready for work at exactly the moment when a Kenny Rogers song played on the radio. What was that all about?

I began to suspect that she was watching out for me. One night, our TV turned on in the middle of the night with that loud, blaring static. It scared us both, but I just looked at my husband and we both said, "It's her." To really find out for sure, I prayed for a sign that she was one of my guides now. The very next day, when I got home from school, I turned on the TV and *The Oprah Winfrey Show* was on. I could never watch that show live, but I would tape it and watch later. I normally had so much to do after I got home, so I would start supper or pick up the kids. This day, I came home and for some reason, I turned on the TV and it was 4:57. That meant Oprah was almost over, and Kenny Rogers was belting out a song to end her show. I was so stunned! I began laughing and shouting, "I knew it!"

This was my sign, and it was even more of a sign since I never turned on the TV right when I got home. She has been with me for many years now, and I still think of her each day and thank her for her help. This, I consider to be the blessing amid all of the pain. I would later learn so much more about death and how we sometimes choose to help others learn their lessons needed by sacrificing ourselves. I believe she did this to become a guide and help all of her loved ones. She was selfless on earth and is now in heaven as well. I feel her energy very specifically, and anytime a Kenny Rogers song comes on, I know it is her. I think back to the radio playing his songs on our trip to search for her body. She was trying to let me know even then, I think.

I learned some valuable lessons from her murder. Grief comes in so many forms, but death is not the end. My belief has become that we are living in but one dimension of many, and these dimensions are vibratory in nature. To the normal people who are not genius physicists, we have learned that they have evidence of the existence of many more dimensions than just the three we know about here on earth. The other side, as some call it, or where we go when we pass this existence, is but another dimension. The dimensions are so close to us, but our vibration is not the same, so we cannot see the others.

One physicist I heard talking on television suggested that the dimension where people might pass through when they die is not up in the sky where we often look when we think of heaven; instead, it is right in front of our faces. This made so much sense to me and had a profound effect on helping to shape my new beliefs about death and dying.

This belief does not diminish the grief; it just changes the perspective. It is helpful to know that when loved ones die, we will see those people again. All they have done is changed their physical form into a spiritual one. They are with us and even help us. Some even try to communicate with us. That does not mean we don't miss them, but it is helpful to know they are there. I think they would want us to know how beautiful it is where they are and that they are happy and healthy. They would want us to know they are home now and can't wait to see us again. Time helps, but as I would learn later, sometimes this point of view is not enough to combat the overwhelming pull of a grief so great that your very being is changed.

I cannot wait to see her again and thank her for all the guidance and love she has shown me in spirit form. In the meantime, I will honor her memory by listening to Kenny Rogers and remembering all the fun times (even the day she caught my then future husband and I in a very compromising situation on the couch in our college apartment. She was supposed to be at work. That is still too fresh, even after thirty-five years, and I am still mortified, while she is probably laughing her head off.) Again, children of mine, I know you are horrified as you read this, and I apologize. We were not saints as we always told you we were.

CHAPTER EIGHT

You Can Take Him Back Now

Parenting is the easiest thing in the world to have an opinion about, but the hardest thing in the world to do.
—*Matt Walsh*

Three years after Shelley was born, a handsome little boy we named Matthew graced our presence. I had the same problems with pre-labor and went to bed once again for a few months. I found myself a good substitute teacher at school and waited it out. Everything went quite well—until we brought him home. Our three-year-old princess loved him—for about a day. Then she announced to us that she was finished playing with him now and we could take him back. We were astounded and had to hold in our laughter as we tried to explain that he was here to stay. You would have thought that she had just been told that Santa, the Tooth Fairy, and the Easter Bunny were all phonies. Imagine the horror!

For the next year, we were so worried by her behavior that we contacted my husband's cousin who happened to be a psychologist. He said she was suffering from separation anxiety because we had put her in a local day care and she was reacting to our attention being divided now between her and the new baby. It was moments like this that we wished that kids came with directions.

We did exactly what the psychologist told us to. We gave her control over little things like her choosing her own clothes, books, and toys and little things like that. The idea was that it would give her some semblance of control in her life. Well, it worked out okay, but it was a day-at-a-time situation.

One day, I got a call from her day care, and she had just begged the UPS man to take her with him. What? Obviously, we had more work to do.

Meanwhile, we were not sleeping at all. Our new son did not know the meaning of the word *sleep*. It seemed we had to be holding him in order for him to sleep. I know there are parents out there with those problems that can relate to our exhaustion. We both had full-time jobs. I honestly don't know how I made it each day teaching all day and then coming home to two children under the age of three with no sleep and seemingly insurmountable problems with each one. We decided sleep was no longer an option, so we consulted the pediatrician. He told us to put our son in his crib at bedtime, shut the door, and let him cry. We were so desperate that we tried it, and it was hard—for one night. It actually worked. He cried about fifteen minutes the first night, and then the second night, it was about five minutes, and then it was smooth sailing from then on. Even our daughter adjusted better the older she got. I guess she finally realized that he was here to stay.

When our son, Matt, was three years old, we had some seriously bizarre conversations with him. Once, while he was sitting on the living room floor playing with his cars, we heard him say that he missed Jesus. My husband and I looked at each other like, did we miss something? We showed no shock or surprise and decided to just let him talk. Matt said he really enjoyed his walks with Jesus because he held his hand. He went on to say that he was so glad that he chose us as his parents. He was lucky, but he sure would like to see Jesus again. Wow, just wow!

There was no way to explain this in a rational way. He was only three years old! Luckily, by that time, I had been immersing myself in books about past lives and predestination. Could it be he really was in heaven before he came here? Could it be he really did choose us as his parents? Could he have agreed to the life lessons he was to learn in this lifetime before he came here? Did it mean the same for all of us? We questioned him, and he was very open with us, not even hesitating to think about his answers. I was convinced he believed this and was telling his truth.

As he grew older, he didn't surprise us as often. However, there was one instance when we were driving out in the country, like we loved to do. He pointed to a crossroads that had fields on all four sides and he said, "That looks like the place where I died. I was fifteen." Needless to say, that took us all by surprise. He was still pretty little, and we had not made a big deal about his other conversations because we wanted them to continue. We also wanted him to not feel bad about sharing things like this with us. So, again, could it be he was remembering his own death? Years later, he would confide in us that he was somewhat fearful the whole year he was fifteen because he thought he was going to die again. That is heavy for a fifteen-year-old to deal with, and I wish he had told us.

We told him about his "heaven" comments when we thought he was old enough to handle it. We were very curious to see if he had any additional thoughts or comments he was keeping to himself. Apparently, he didn't, and he also did not recall his previous comments. I had no real answers to explain his behavior, but it did cement my belief that there is another part of us hidden in our soul that remembers all of our past experiences. It seems as we mature as children, these past life memories fade and become buried in our subconscious mind. We just grow up, and society implores us to hide it and bury it deep. I feel that if we openly remembered, we would heal much more easily. Perhaps that is part of the lesson. Nobody said it was going to be easy.

CHAPTER NINE

Special Person, Special Place

*Some people come into our lives and quickly go.
Some stay for a while, leave footprints on our
hearts, and we are never, ever the same.*
—*Flavia Weedn*

How rare is it to find a person who, upon entering your life, changes it for the better? I believe there could possibly be another woman out there who is completely and utterly selfless. I am sure there has to be another mom that loves her sons so deeply that she can't fathom life without them. I know that somewhere in the world, another female exists for the sole purpose of loving her grandchildren. There probably is another woman somewhere on this earth that accepts her daughter-in-law with unconditional love. Surely, there is a lady out there who is so very generous with her time and efforts. The world just has to have a mom that cooks and bakes elaborate meals solely for the purpose of sharing that gift with her family. But I've never met another woman with all those qualities, except for one: my mother-in-law, Betty. Yep, I won the mother-in-law lottery. She accepted me from the moment her son took me to meet her and I spilled iced tea all over myself. She has been there for me through all the good and bad times.

She was there when I married her son and welcomed me with open arms. She was there for me when I asked her to help me keep my children safely far away from the person who had abused me. She kept both the kids while I taught and so I needed to make sure there were only two people with my permission to keep my children alone, and that was her and my own mom. Nobody else was allowed to keep them by themselves. My children were to never know the word *abuse* at any time in their lives. I would die first. She understood that because she felt the same way, so it was no big surprise that she helped me out. She was there crying with me when we lost her first grandchild. She was there to rock her granddaughter in the ICU after emergency surgery to save her life. She was there when we needed someone to keep our daughter while we helped search for my missing friend. She was there for me at the following funeral by keeping my kids for me. She was there to welcome my son to this world and to try to explain to my daughter why we had to keep him. She was there every weekend to make us the best meals ever to be found on this planet. She was there to see all of her grandchildren graduate from high school. She was there for me when they left for college. She knew how I felt. She was there when my mom died, and I told her that she had to be my mom now, but then I realized that she always had been. Thank you, Mom.

That very special person would lead me to a very special place. When I met my husband, his parents lived in an idyllic little village with a beautiful, swiftly flowing creek running right through their property. We loved going to their house on weekends. Our children have so many fond memories of the time spent with their grandmamma by the creek. Their cousins were about the same age, and when they all got together, it was fun for everyone.

As the town grew up around them, my in-laws were feeling smothered. When they moved there in the early 60s, it was in the country. When offered a tidy sum to sell in the late 90s, they accepted and found a couple hundred acres really in the country. We lovingly still refer to the new place as "the ranch." Talk about memories. When the kids were still young, we would have picnics by the creek running right through the middle of the ranch. They grew up riding in the Gator, which was a four-wheeler that could carry up to four people. We would often go spotlighting at night searching for animals. It was great fun, especially when their dad told ghost stories. My daughter learned where not to step when she found herself knee deep in cow patties. I still remember gagging as I washed her off in the creek.

The ranch was therapeutic for me. When I had a bad week at work, all I would have to do was enter the front gate and I instantly relaxed. It was better than chocolate, wine, and a bubble bath by candlelight all put together. Grant knew what I wanted to do. I always, without fail, wanted to ride in the Gator over every square inch of trails on the property, and we had plenty of trails. It usually took an afternoon, but it was glorious. The wind in my hair and the fresh air was like medicine for my soul. Nature is a great healer, or even *the* great healer. It is tragic that the children of today are so nature-deprived. Even as recently as sixty to seventy years ago, nature was just a part of existence. People benefited without knowing what they were getting. We only know now because most people aren't enjoying nature's positive benefits, and when they do get out for a day, they wonder why they didn't come outside sooner.

There is just a special connection we have with nature. Grant always says, "To know nature is to know God." Everything in nature has God's fingerprints on it, from a leaf on a plant to a cloud in the sky. Being in nature automatically raises your vibration, which calms you down and makes you happy. To many, including my nature nerd of a husband, being in nature is a spiritual experience. He thinks that being in nature can be a truly spiritual event. It can be strange for the novice that has never been out, but if you can imagine that all things seen, smelled, touched, and sometimes even tasted are directly linked to God's spirit without any adulterated influences of humans, one can truly know and appreciate God's presence in the world. If you don't get out much, try it. Go for a drive in the country, ride a bike, or go to a state park. I promise you that you will be glad you did.

CHAPTER TEN

More Learning than Teaching

*The woman who does not require validation from
anyone is the most feared individual on the planet.*
—Mohadesa Najumi

We are constantly learning. Whether we know it or not, we learn more than we don't learn. Earth is our classroom. True healing comes from learning the lessons we are here to learn.

I taught elementary school for more years than I didn't teach elementary school. That's eye-opening even as I write it. I can say unequivocally that I learned something new all throughout my days of teaching. Most of the lessons I learned came from the kids themselves.

I knew I wanted to be a teacher at a very early age, and I worked toward that goal through my teen and young adult years.

Up until we lost Sarah, my career was not going like I'd planned. I was put in schools where discipline was only a wish that never came true. The students were so troubled, and I was so young and inexperienced that I did not have the tools I needed to make an impact on them. This was very evident when I returned to school in January after Sarah died in mid-December and one particularly troubled fourth grader laughed at me and told me he was glad my baby died. That was it for me. I walked out of the classroom and up to the principal's office and resigned.

I returned to the classroom several months after Shelley was born. I requested only certain schools, and I was sticking to my guns. I scored an interview and found my dream job at one of the top schools in town. I entered that new phase of my life hell bent on one thing: I would do my job to the best of my ability, but when it came time to go home each day, I was a mom. Even though my mom and mother-in-law kept my daughter, I still ached inside to be with her. The guilt I felt over leaving her was enormous and hard to overcome. It was only when she was grown that I would allow myself to forgive my having to work and not stay home with her. Today she is a bright, beautiful, and independent young woman. She is so happy, and that makes me happy. My coworkers, especially the ones whose life was their job, did not agree with my philosophy of leaving on time and not staying until late in the evening. This would provide fuel for another guilt trip.

Teaching was an important part of my life but not the most important. Somehow, I was able to get it all done and do a pretty super job while balancing home and work. I often teased that all I needed was a red cape because I felt like Superwoman most of the time.

As the years went on and Matt was born and they both started school, it became easier. They attended the elementary school where I taught, and I loved having them there—most of the time. I even taught both of them in third grade. Those years were awkward, and I bent over backward to remain unbiased to the point of being too hard on them, I think. We made it through, and when they started middle school, I breathed a small sigh of relief.

I was so lucky through the rest of my career, because I had, without a doubt, the best principals ever to tackle the job. I had to help my coworkers "break-in" about six different principals over thirty years, but we managed to do it easily because they were, simply put, great people.

Some principals pushed me to excel in the classroom and develop some much-needed self-confidence by planning and organizing speaking engagements for me. It became laughable, and I always knew something was up when she would just pop in and ask me for a "favor." One favor was playing host to the commissioner of education for the state of Texas. I was to teach a lesson on character to my third-graders while literally every dignitary in the district and town were present, along with the commissioner and local media. It turned out great, but I was a nervous wreck preparing for it. I would get e-mails from some principals in the early morning hours when they should have been asleep, like 2:00 a.m. They were all so dedicated. One principal led our school to its first-ever exemplary rating. Our school also happened to be the first one in the city to get this distinguished honor. It took hard work and a team effort, but I can say that we would not have done it without our principal. She is now a superintendent in another district, and I am sure she still impresses everyone.

My last principal was by far the one I appreciated the most. He was the most understanding person I have ever met. He was there for the children, and that was his priority. Every decision he made was based on that fact. Later on, when I began to get restless, he encouraged me to take a higher position. That position required our collaboration in the form of weekly meetings and impromptu ones as well. Those talks meant a lot to me and helped me to do my job better. We always seemed to be on the same page about things. Perhaps the best thing I appreciated about him was that he knew family came first, so if any teacher ever needed to be with his or her children, he was the first to say "go home," no matter how difficult it was to find a replacement. He is still at school every morning by 6:00 a.m. to see the children off the buses and make sure they receive a warm welcome. He is retiring this year. There will never be anyone who can fill his shoes, although someone will be waiting to try. I hope that person succeeds.

People have those days in their workplace that are hard to handle and make coming to work seem like drudgery. Many feel stuck inside a job that does not make them happy, but they feel they have no choice but to stay. Many love their job, but the people they work with grate on their last nerve. Many cannot accept authority, let alone follow the rules of a boss. Many know that they are meant for something more than their current job but do not know what to do about it. Still others know their passion but feel there is no money to be made doing it.

Big issues revolve around the workplace. I was so lucky to have escaped any real issues for many years, but that would change when I worked toward a job outside of the classroom. I wanted to work with teachers on the best strategies to use in the classroom and help them find the materials to do their jobs with excellence. I went through a lot of coursework and had to give up many a weekend to prepare myself for the new job, but I felt I was ready for this change.

I experienced great success with my students, particularly in the areas of reading and writing, and that was reflected on state tests. So I was overjoyed when I got the job as literacy coordinator on my campus. I loved it! Those were some of the happiest years for me. However, I ran into problems that blindsided me.

I found out that I had a couple of coworkers spreading not-so-nice rumors about me. The funny thing was that I found out while conducting an after-school in-service. One of the teachers in the class came up to me as we were all getting ready to leave and shared with me that I had a couple of people on my campus that were not my biggest fans. It seems that, according to them, I didn't put in enough hours and was not doing the job like it was supposed to be done. I knew in my heart that they were speaking to the fact that they thought they could do the job better. One of them had wanted the job and openly campaigned for it. It went to me, and even though she never said a word, I knew she must be feeling angry. This was how it was playing out, and I had to deal. It must be said, at this point, that I am a perfectionist when it comes to my work and other things as well. It also must be added that I am a peacemaker, which means I avoid confrontation, and in my world, everyone must get along. So, needless to say, rumors about me, on my own campus, pretty near destroyed me.

I had been on that campus twenty years, and my reputation was invaluable to me. I did not know what to do. I had many supporters, but I could see the campus dividing. I had to do something—and fast. I decided to talk with one of the two teachers that had instigated the rumors. I was so nervous. Confrontation was not in my area of comfort at all. I decided to just tell it like it was and let her know how I felt. I also wanted to know why she and her friend felt the way they did. Had I done something wrong? The meeting did not go well. She was defensive the moment I walked through the door. Oh boy! This was not going away. I came to the conclusion that a person's basic personality cannot be changed.

Every person has dark, shadowy parts that sometimes control his or her actions. Some people have deep and hurtful pasts that fuel their future in negative ways. They take it out on others, when, in reality, it has nothing at all to do with their victims. I knew this, and it helped me to get through the days with the stares and whispers of my detractors.

If people don't want to change or don't see the havoc they are creating, then the behaviors will not change. It becomes a recovery rather than a rescue.

I had to adjust my reaction and consider my next steps carefully so the campus could be healed and no further damage done to lower morale. I spent each day going about my business and being nice and supportive, even to those I knew were being hateful. I prayed for unity on my campus and the healing of the ones who were so hurt that they had to lash out at others for control. Fortunately for me, as I was at my wit's end, they both moved to a different campus. I didn't know why, and I didn't want to know why. My nightmare was over, but the effects lingered like a dark cloud.

I had begun to doubt my abilities in that job. I found myself questioning my own commitment to it, and I completely talked myself into believing I was not the right person for the job anymore. I was experiencing burnout, but I still had several years before I could retire. I found another job on the same campus, and it gave me complete joy for the remaining years up until my retirement.

What are the blessings to be found when people you thought were your friends turn on you and say hateful things that cut you deep? How do you come out of it a better and more confident person? My blessing came when all of that trouble led me to take a job that would make me yearn to come to school and thankfully made my burnout only a memory.

After twenty-five years, I found that my favorite thing was teaching first-graders how to read. Had I known that earlier on, things would have been different. Again, the hard times crafted my personality into that of a more assertive and cautious person. I would need and use these skills later in my life. The whole experience taught me a lot about people and what motivates them to do the things they do. I learned some valuable lessons about my own ways of dealing with conflict. The peacemaker in me wanted to run and hide and not step foot in school again. I had to man up and find a way to deal—and I did.

It helped me when I realized that the ones hurting me were on their own journey. I did not have to understand it or like it. I just had to accept it. Frankly, I would never want that type of person for a friend anyway. It has not escaped my attention that I have not seen them since they left my campus, but I did hear that they were very sorry and regretted all the conflict. Sorry to say, they never contacted me to tell me that. That is also part of their journey and not mine. My part is to forgive them.

For all the peacemakers out there, I know what you are going through day in and day out trying to keep everyone happy. It is literally exhausting. It became a real burden for me when the job of making sure everyone got along became increasingly harder to accomplish. It seems I had to be peacemaker at home as well as school, as you can imagine with two teenagers. Sometimes I felt like I was on duty 24-7. I became so tired of this thankless job of preserving peace that I decided to take ownership of my own power and try to become more assertive.

This whole concept of owning your power has some of the most basic spiritual philosophies behind it. Since we are all God's children and were made in his image, then we are extensions of that divinity. Since God is omnipotent and omnipresent, he has unlimited power. As daughters and sons of God, we possess that same unlimited power. Power is, simply put, an energy that allows us to influence outcomes. If you own your power, you are in charge of your life. If you do not own your power, then life is in charge of you. I needed to learn how to become a person who used power to the benefit of not only me but also of all those around me.

I had always wanted to live so that if anything bad was ever said about me, nobody would believe it. I needed to take charge and carefully craft each and every day. I needed to stand up for myself and learn the word *no*. I know there are a lot of people who need to learn this word as well. After trying it out, I felt so liberated and, well, powerful. It was a grand feeling and one I wanted to keep. I even found it helpful to just get up and walk away when others started being negative or confrontational. It was my own passive way of communicating that I was not going to sit there and listen to it.

What I found was astonishing and so simple. When faced with no audience to play in front of, those wanting to argue simply stopped. I quickly learned that it was all about control. So many things are rooted in this deep need for control. Rather than try to heal the reason for the disagreement, which could be trivial in nature, the real healing would be dealing with the control issue.

I learned that there is a nice way to exert your control without exploding in someone's face. To me, that is not our true power. The power is getting our point across without any negative consequences. Emotions are sticky things that fuel all of our actions and reactions. It would serve us all well to examine our own motivations and deal with the emotions behind them. I can't say for certain that the sugary-sweet, passive peacemaker who kept the peace by gently talking everyone down is gone, but her appearances are getting more rare.

CHAPTER ELEVEN

The Tornado

You never know how strong you are until being
strong is the only choice you have.
—*Bob Marley*

We all have those times in life that just happen so suddenly that we have no control over them, but they change your life forever. I had such an event occur many years ago near the town where I lived. At the time, I was a third-grade teacher at a public elementary school and both of my children attended with me.

One particular day, when taking my students out to recess, I noticed immediately upon going outside that it was like stepping into an oven. It was also like I had stepped into a painting or something ethereal. The way it looked outside was like nothing I had ever seen before. Everything looked a shade of green that I cannot describe. It was late May, so green was normal, but something was different. I don't even have words for it. It almost appeared not of this world. We played for just a few minutes because it was so hot. The children were complaining, so we went in. About thirty minutes later, the tornado drill came over the loud speaker. It was a series of bells, and we all knew the protocol for what to do from our regular practice drills. We all thought it was just another drill.

We got all of the children out in the hallway and had them kneel and clasp their hands behind their heads. We thought the drill was taking a while longer than usual when we heard the storm sirens blaring outside. Our town had several sirens spread throughout that were tested every Saturday morning at 11:00, so we knew this was not a test. They had never gone off before other than on Saturday.

One of my fellow teachers had a radio in her room, so she went and turned it on to see what was going on. As I look back, I wonder why our principal didn't keep us more informed, but she was very busy taking calls from worried parents. The radio said that there was a tornado outbreak, which meant that there were several tornadoes in the area that were heading directly toward us. Some had even morphed into each other and produced even bigger tornadoes that were as wide as a mile.

The sirens had not stopped and just continued blaring. The children were getting scared and were tired of kneeling. We let them rest for intervals while listening to the radio. It seemed like the whole town was just waiting for the worst to happen. It seemed inevitable. Some parents came and picked their kids up, but it was hard to keep track. I kept a list of my children and when they left and with whom. My own two children were in second and fifth grades. My second-grader, Matt, was terrified, so I sent for his big sister to see if she could calm him down. We tried to get other siblings together as best we could. I was so glad I was not a kindergarten teacher, because that campus wing of students was hysterical! We ended up being in the hall for around five hours. It all began about 12:30 just after lunch, and the last child remaining in my class left at 5:00. It was bedlam, to say the least.

Our town did not take a direct hit, thank goodness, but several nearby towns did. Storm damage was everywhere due to the high winds, and power lines were down as well.

I finally got home with my kids only to realize that the biggest tornado, a mile and a half wide, had crossed near our ranch fifteen miles from where we lived. We owned this with my husband's parents, but nobody lived on the property. We had animals out there, though.

When Grant arrived home, we decided to drive out to the ranch just to check on the animals and see if any damage had been done to the property.

When we got to the main county road, which led to another road where our property was, it was blocked by literally dozens of emergency vehicles. We saw helicopters hovering and wondered what was going on. We could not get to our road the usual way, so we decided to try a back road, because by this time, we were really concerned.

When we turned onto the back road, my life, as I knew it at that time, changed in just one brief moment. When I look back on it, I see it in slow motion. One of these days, I am going to investigate what this slow-motion thing is, because it happens a lot to me during certain experiences. Once we turned onto the alternate back road, the sights we saw would make even the strongest person sick. We saw cows—or what was left of them—literally wrapped around broken telephone poles. We saw numerous body parts that we could only assume were from animals, but we would later learn they could have been human remains. We saw a tractor in a tree—one of the only trees still standing. We saw no vegetation, no grass at all in the tornado's path. It was just dirt where green fields used to be. The road we traveled on had no pavement anymore; the surface was gone. We saw horses ripped apart. I immediately started crying and feeling sick to my stomach. My husband was quiet, and then I thought, *Oh no, my kids have just seen this. They will be scarred for life.* So I said, rather loudly, "Kids, get down in the floorboard and cover your heads until we get off this road." My son immediately went down and did as he was told, gratefully. My daughter, ever like her father, was like, "Look at that; did you see that?" She was mesmerized and not at all shook up like her mother. Like I said, she is her father's daughter.

We could not go any further because there were roadblocks everywhere. We now knew why, or so we thought. Our ranch would just have to wait until we could reach it. We could see the path that the tornado had taken because there was literally nothing, and then on either side of the path, there was vegetation again. We hoped ours had been spared.

We still had to get back to town to attend a long-planned school function. Ugh! I was a complete and utter wreck. I somehow pulled it together and was able to tell a few people what we saw, when we learned that the small community where our ranch was located in Jarrell, Texas, had lost an entire subdivision. Twenty-six people were unaccounted for and presumed dead. There were no houses left, only foundations, and even those were spotty.

We would later learn that this tornado was an F5, the worst on the scale that measures tornado strength. I wondered where all those people went, and where were their belongings, like their refrigerators or dryers? Silly, but really, those things weigh a lot. Some people did survive. One lady hid in her bathtub and ended up in a tree. Many were not so lucky. There was an entire family of five that was lost. Remains and belongings would be found on nearby property for months to come, and some were never found, just vanished into thin air, just like that. I could not get it out of my head. Along with everyone else, I was desperate for more news each day. We all hoped that someone would be found alive that was missing. None of the missing were ever found alive.

Eerily, three days later, we found ourselves under another tornado warning. Our household went nuts. We were all scared. I wondered what the people felt like that had lived through the horror just three days earlier. I could only wonder what terror they must feel even today when bad weather approaches.

Thankfully, all was okay and has been since. Our ranch was spared, but all of the grass was pressed down lying to one side due to the intense winds. It was eerie to see the path the tornado had taken. It came within a quarter of a mile of our property. The town built a memorial to the victims, and many survivors rebuilt on that same street, but there was and still is to this day a big demand for storm shelters. That is a day I will never forget.

I often think of that tornado and wonder what God's plan was for that community. What about natural disasters? I have more questions than answers about those subjects, and I figure I will until I get to heaven and can ask them.

What are the lessons or blessings, or is there anything one can take away from such a terrible disaster? I believe I was changed so that I would have empathy for people who go through things like that. My young son, even at age seven, learned the same lesson. He had five dollars and wanted to donate it to the Red Cross, so we went to the place in town where they were accepting donations and let him make his. I am sure he will never forget that, and neither will we, because we were both proud of his decision to help.

Many of us felt that way when we heard about other natural disasters, like the tsunami in Indonesia or the earthquake in Japan, or, most recently, the many tornadoes in our states.

So what do we do? We give to help those in need. We raise money. We donate clothing and other immediate needs. We pray and pray and pray for healing and help for those afflicted. That is what God wants us to do. I believe that each of our souls' purpose for being on earth is to help others, any way we can. It doesn't have to be big to help. It doesn't have to be money to help. There are so many ways to help others. There are even ways to help others that only require a smile when someone is having a bad day or an ear to listen to a friend in need. These are all ways to help that are more powerful than people realize.

Have you ever entered a room and someone was so glad to see you that they smiled big and came your way to talk or give you a hug? This is an energetic exchange. It is just another way of helping people. You are sharing your positive energy with them. The list is endless. For me personally, I have always been drawn to helping children, and being a teacher helped me see where the needs were. I also live near a very large military base, and I see a need to help those soldiers coming home to readjust in any way that is possible.

One way people can help is to donate items they don't use anymore. Several places take donations and will even give you a receipt to use for a tax deduction.

I used to think that the panhandlers on the side of the road that held up those signs that said they were homeless and without work were just trolling for their next dollar to buy liquor. I know a lot of people feel this way. However, I have changed my thoughts about this, because it is not our place to judge those people. It is our place to help them. So, if you feel like they might not spend money wisely, offer them a sandwich, a coupon, the paper to search for jobs—it doesn't matter what they do with what you give them. That is their journey. What matters is what you did to help someone else, and that is your journey.

One of the biggest lessons I have learned in my so-called journey is that everyone is on his or her own personal journey of soul development, even your spouse and children. It is not your journey; it is theirs. Your journey, or job, is to help them along the way on theirs. Sometimes that involves letting your loved ones make their own mistakes so they can learn the lessons they are here to learn. You cannot bail out everyone you love or you will become an enabler, and they will never learn their lessons. This is a hard pill to swallow for parents, but I believe after your children reach a certain age, it is time to let them learn for themselves, and hopefully you have given them all the tools they will need to make wise choices.

I will close my personal soapbox on helping by saying that I believe most people don't realize how the small things they do on a daily basis can be of help to others. I once read a suggestion that at any given moment in time, you should think about how you can help any person have a better day. It can be a person on the street, in the car next to you, or in the line at the grocery store. It is so simple, yet so profound.

CHAPTER TWELVE

Dis-ease

❦

Fear does not stop death. It stops life.
—Rickson Gracie

You have probably heard the saying, "If momma ain't happy, nobody's happy," or "Happy wife, happy life." In a way, there is some truth to this. If you were to ask my husband, he would say, without blinking, it is entirely true. This was hammered home to me when my life dramatically changed—for the better.

I had suffered for years with a misdiagnosis of irritable bowel syndrome. I would get debilitating stomach pains. The horrible bowel problems that would inevitably follow an attack just magically went away after a brief period of time, until they would return again. I had been suffering since high school, but it was getting worse.

One night, I had an attack in the middle of the night. It was way worse than any attack I'd had up to that point, which meant it was unbearable. I debated going to the emergency room, but locally, ours had a horrible reputation of unfathomable long waits. I knew I could not do that. Finally, after waiting for it to go away, like it always did, I came to the realization that it was not going away. I woke my husband, who took the decision from me, and we quickly got ready to go to the ER. When we arrived, they took one look at me, examined my symptoms, and I bypassed all the waiting. They did a test that I don't ever tell people I had because it is so embarrassing. It confirmed that my intestines were "kinked," and they were not correcting themselves like they normally did. I would experience tissue death if I did not have emergency surgery. So, I went into surgery at 1:00 a.m. with a diagnosis of probably coming out with a colostomy bag. If I had prayed before this point, my prayers were now on steroids. As it turned out, doctors removed 30 percent of my colon, and I did not need a colostomy bag. Thank God!

My recovery was long, but my stomach issues disappeared overnight! It was revealed to me that I never had IBS. What I had been experiencing were my intestines kinking and then correcting themselves. I had put up with that for decades and been misdiagnosed all that time. Ironically, it was some new medication I was trying that brought on the attack that quite literally saved my life.

About a week or two after the surgery, I got a late-night call from the pathologist that tested the tissue from the surgery. It was routine to do this, although I did not realize the pathologist tests were being done at the time on me. He informed me that during surgery, they had found a tumor in my appendix. They decided to remove the appendix entirely. Testing on the tumor proved it was precancerous. He told me that if given a few years, the tumor would have become malignant. It would have been hard to find and diagnose before it spread to other areas. I could not speak. I was so shocked, but extremely grateful. He informed me that a colonoscopy was being scheduled so they could make sure there were no other issues. Reluctantly, I consented to the colonoscopy. I knew it was important, but I had heard horror stories about colonoscopies. I will spare you my gruesome experience with it only to say that everything was fine and no abnormalities were found.

It was hard to wrap my mind around the events that led to this experience. The only explanation had to be divine intervention. God works in mysterious ways, doesn't he? How awesome it is to experience how he truly takes care of us. We should be thanking him profusely on a daily basis for all the wonderful things we have, instead of complaining about all that is wrong. This is the basis for positive thinking and is the most powerful manifesting tool you can ever have.

A byproduct of my surgery was that I lost ten pounds. I wasn't obese, but I could stand to lose some. I decided that this opportunity only rolled around once in a lifetime and I needed to capitalize on it. I had a good friend who had lost a ton of weight by cutting out carbs, and her transformation was motivation enough for me to give it a try. I had also invested in a Pilates video and was anxious to try it out, so I put the two together and began my wellness program. Eight weeks later, I was twenty-six pounds down. I was completely transformed.

It may sound shallow, but my life literally changed because of my physical transformation. I enjoyed clothes shopping like never before, and I totally loved makeup and all the girly stuff. As a consequence, I began to spend a little more time and take care of myself. Before, I was all about the kids and my job, taking very little time for myself.

Part of that new self-love thing I had going on was emphatically refusing to allow my hair to go gray. I cannot remember my mom when she didn't have gray hair, obviously going gray prematurely. I had inherited that tendency. That meant I needed to find someone who could repair the rat's nest I called my hair.

Fate is so funny. I called a hairdresser that had been referred to me, but she refused to color my hair, stating that this was not her specialty. She referred me to another girl named Alicia, so I made an appointment with her.

That was a true God set-up because not only did Alicia completely transform my hair, she also became a dear friend. A dear friend who was on her own spiritual journey that mirrored my own. I didn't realize how great it was to be in the company of someone who was like-minded and freely shared her thoughts. We have great conversations, and nothing is off-limits. She has true spiritual gifts that she tries to understand and manage. I hope I have helped her come to terms with her gifts as she has helped me.

It goes without saying that she alone is responsible for the great hair I have. It has nothing to do with me. She taught me the proper way to take care of my hair. She also taught me different ways to fix it and the best products to use. This added onto the self-esteem boost I had going on from losing weight. A piece of advice: do not ever take for granted the value of a talented hairdresser. That stuff is important.

I felt so good about myself, better than I had ever in my whole life. It was liberating and quite surprising to me. If I had known I could feel this way by losing some weight, taking care of myself, and changing my hair, I would have done it a long time ago.

Needless to say, this newfound happiness spilled over into my family life. Things magically changed for the better. Everyone seemed happier, and we got even closer as a family unit. My energy was contagious, and I was more than happy to share it.

This experience was a great healer. It introduced me to the concept of self-love and how important it is. I believe it is a major life lesson that we are all here to learn.

How do you practice self-love? What does it even mean? After researching this topic, I had to agree that, historically, I had not been practicing self-love at all. In fact, I had been doing the opposite. I was mired in self-criticism, always believing the bad about myself. I never tried too hard on my appearance, believing that it wouldn't do me any good anyway. I found that loving yourself does not mean being arrogant, vain, or selfish. It is self-acceptance, self-approval, and self-worth. It can be demonstrated by us keeping our bodies healthy, creating an organized and clean home, being responsible for wise money decisions, and steering clear of creating burdens for ourselves.

When we criticize ourselves, mistreat our bodies, procrastinate about things that would benefit us, and allow loved ones to abuse and belittle us, we are not loving ourselves.

Louise Hay has written many books, but my favorite is *You Can Heal Your Life*. She discusses self-love at length as part of a way that we can heal ourselves. It is well worth the effort for us to work on this aspect of ourselves. Once this lesson is learned, miracles can really happen.

Years after the surgery, I stumbled upon a philosophy that intrigued me and made me completely rethink illness. I felt a calling to read *A Course in Miracles*. It states that, "All dis-ease comes from a state of unforgiveness. Whenever we are ill, we need to look around and see who it is we need to forgive." We don't have to know how; we just have to let it go. Louise Hay said, "The very person you find it hardest to forgive is the one you need to let go of the most." Her philosophy is that dis-ease can be healed if we are willing to change the way we think, believe, and act.

At any given moment in time, we are either acting out of love or fear. Fear can be a root cause of illness. If everything is energy and energy can be changed and converted, why can't this include the energy of healing an illness? I would never in a million years substitute this for a doctor's care. If I were really sick, or I had a broken bone, I would be the first to go to the doctor, but I was curious. I knew that people could literally think themselves sick. If that is the case, then we can certainly think ourselves well. Some of the physical aches and pains we have, we bring on ourselves in our mind by the way we think. I pondered over this for a time while I read Hay's book. When I saw a chart of illnesses along with the emotion behind them that needed to be healed, it made sense. For example, my stomach problems could be explained emotionally by addressing what it was that I could not stomach. Well, since the illness began with me at a young age, I can only conclude that it was the abuse I needed to let go of and forgive. That clearly tells us who we need to forgive or the issue that we need to heal. Would the stomach issue simply go away if the emotions were addressed? I believe so, but why not combine a doctor's expertise in conjunction with your own emotional healing? This is a very short and simple explanation of a very complex issue, but it makes perfect sense. It is an interesting concept, but not a new one. Either way, it holds great potential for self-healing.

Life goes on, even in the midst of spiritual epiphanies. Shortly after my surgery, Matt earned his Eagle Scout ranking. That tremendous accomplishment was a family effort. We were so proud and knew this was one of those rare resume-enhancing events.

We had a couple of really super kids. I will be the first to say that luck had nothing to do with it. We worked hard on a daily basis to parent both kids as best as we could. As the years flew by, both excelled in various pursuits. We found ourselves always going to school functions, plays, band rehearsals, football practices, soccer practices, and flute lessons. We attended every concert, game, play, and teacher meeting. They graduated, and both were accepted into the colleges that they selected. We were now entering a new phase for everyone.

CHAPTER THIRTEEN

Empty Nest, Or What Am I Going to Do Now?

Some people are old at 18 and some are young at 90 ... time is a concept that humans created.
—Yoko Ono

I thought that my daughter leaving home for college was hard, but I didn't know hard until my son left and there I was left staring at some man I had called husband for twenty-seven years.

What got me the most was the silence. Lucky for me, I still had my job to keep me busy. I would just throw myself into it and this empty, hollow feeling would pass. Only it didn't pass. I found myself questioning everything about the rest of my life and the direction in which I wanted it to go.

Compounding this problem was the fact that my son had just joined the Corps of Cadets program at our alma mater, Texas A&M University. Don't get me wrong, we were overjoyed that he got into that particular university, especially as part of the Fightin' Texas Aggie Band, but I was uneasy with what I knew he would be facing in the years to come in the Corps. The program at Texas A&M was all about preparing young men and women toward leadership roles in the various branches of the military upon graduation. Being able to continue to play the drums at the college level was what caught his eye. Luckily, he was only ninety minutes away. We had heard horror stories about the freshman year. The philosophy was that a cadet had to be torn down in order to be built back up and the result would be leadership abilities of a whole new caliber. We could only whisper among other parents about the physical and mental challenges we knew our kids were experiencing daily. We were told to expect our son to call us begging to come home but not to let him. I decided I would not be answering the phone, because I would offer to pick him up myself and buy him a milkshake on the way home. I had not cut the apron strings yet. It was too soon.

Needless to say, the year was beyond tough. It was one of the hardest of my life, not only because of my son's situation, but also because my own personal demons were coming to life in the quiet. One consolation was that we loved Aggie football, so we purchased season tickets and looked forward to every weekend away bolstering him up and enjoying some football. It would take me all week to recuperate from the sweltering temperatures that a hot afternoon football game in Texas could bring, along with the angst our son was going through.

They say that life can change on a dime in a matter of mere seconds, and I had seen that firsthand a number of times, but this time was different. My mother-in-law had a friend that she had met while attending weekly senior citizen lunches. She had lost her son to murder and was having a terrible time coping with her loss, so she decided to see a psychic medium to help her out. She claimed that this therapist gave her peace beyond measure, so my mother-in-law wanted to go and see for herself.

We both had something in common. We longed for spiritual peace that comes from knowledge beyond our understanding. We talked about angels, the hereafter, and whether or not people could actually speak on behalf of those that had passed to the other side. She asked me if I would like to see this person and ask her some questions that she obviously felt would be answered. I jumped at the chance because I was so starved for truth and anything to shed the light on the next phase in my life.

My mother-in-law went in first for thirty minutes, and then I was to follow for the last thirty minutes of the one-hour session. Those thirty minutes passed in a second. I was mesmerized. The woman, Linda Drake, who would become my mentor, was beautiful and cordial. She immediately made me feel at ease. I asked her all sorts of things, and she told me things that she would have no way of knowing. I ended up staying over an hour with her. She told me something that changed the entire course of my life: I was a healer. My purpose in this life was to heal others in whatever way I was led. Wow! I can remember thinking to myself, *When can I come back and talk to her some more?* That one hour started me on years of self-healing and cramming in as much knowledge about healing as I could possibly hold. When I look back on that time of indecision and, truthfully, feeling very lost and alone, I realize Linda was sent to help me find a focus for the rest of my life. I can say that these last eight years since I met her have been the most fulfilling period of growth I have experienced.

Meeting Linda would also lead me to my best friend. I wanted to learn more about this sort of thing, so I found myself signing up for all kinds of classes, both online and in-person workshops. I would travel at night after a day of teaching school and not return until late. I was so energized with my newfound purpose that it didn't matter. One particular workshop focused on people like me who were just starting out on their spiritual journey. We were to learn about angels and delve into some serious philosophical topics about healing. At this class, I sat beside a friendly and beautiful lady named Kathy. Have you ever come into contact with a total stranger and immediately felt a bond that literally came out of nowhere? This is the feeling that rushed into my body. I felt like I had known her forever. We quickly developed a deep friendship that remains today. Our journeys are similar, and we rely on each other for advice and a shoulder to lean on. I value her friendship more than I can put into words.

That first class we attended was perhaps the weirdest thing I have ever experienced. There were about ten of us, all women except for one young man. We had been discussing angels, and as we entered into a guided meditation, one of the young women went completely berserk! She started yelling and telling "them" to go away. She even threw up. At one point, as we were all staring at each other, wondering what in the heck was wrong with her and what we should do, she looked directly at me and said, "They want you to know you are going to be sick around your heart area and you need to get it checked out."

First of all, I wanted to know who "they" were, and then I wanted more details about my heart problem. She said she saw a darkness around either my lungs or heart.

That scared me, so I made an appointment with my doctor. What was I going to tell my doctor? Oh, by the way, a girl, who happens to be psychic, told me she could see that I had a heart problem, and here I am; so tell me, what's wrong with my heart? Crap! I have always believed in the truth, so I told her a small version of it that didn't sound too far off base. I told my doctor that someone who claimed to have "insight" told me I was going to be sick or might already be sick and it had something to do with my heart or lungs. The poor doctor didn't even blink an eye. She ordered an EKG and some blood work. She checked my lungs and gave me a complete physical, remaining professional while I felt so dumb. Everything came back fine. I felt like a total fool! Her next step should've been to refer me to another specialist, say, a psychiatrist. Thankfully, she didn't, and this wonderful, understanding lady is still my doctor.

What was I buying into? Was this my direction and my truth? I certainly did not want to go back to that class, except to visit with Kathy again. Our teacher told us that the student had been gently told to step back and take some time to acclimate. She never returned to class. To be on the safe side, I e-mailed Linda to get her opinion. I told her what had happened and that if that was what happened once you were "enlightened," I really didn't want any part of it. Once again, Mr. Murphy would follow me around. Him and his laws! It turned out Linda was best friends with the teacher of the class. How embarrassing! I sucked it up and continued the classes and enjoyed them immensely and developed many lifelong friends.

It wasn't until several months later that I would learn that spirit does not operate on our timeline. That Thanksgiving while I was caring for my daughter, who had come home from college sick as a dog with the H1N1 virus, I learned that the girl who'd told me I would be getting sick with either a heart or lung problem was right on the money. I contracted the virus the day my daughter left to go back to school. I was so sick that I also got a bad case of double pneumonia. I coughed for months and took antibiotics three different times to get rid of it. It damaged my lungs and I developed asthma, which I had never had before. I have asthma even today because of it. It sure made me think about whether people could actually see or hear messages from those in spirit. I became a believer the longer I studied and learned about this fascinating field of spirit.

By far, the best thing to come out of all the classes was meeting Kathy. Our lives mirrored each other. We each had been married forever and had two kids, a boy and a girl. Unknowingly, we had each begun our journey with the same mentor at the same time. She has been there for me through many trials and listened to me when I know that nobody else would have ever understood. We were both abused as children and had brought our children up shielding them from any trauma. It seemed that we came into this world to learn multiple lessons, and we soon learned that if we were going to heal others, we first had to heal ourselves. That is a journey we remain on and travel together.

For those empty nesters out there, it isn't as much fun as they say, especially at first. Time manages to help in getting us accustomed to a new lifestyle.

I found myself at a spiritual crossroads, which I think had been brewing for many years, but I had just been too busy being supermom to see it. I can remember crying to my mom that I felt like I needed to go to church, but no church seemed to fit what I felt I needed.

Every book I read and person I talked to emphasized the importance of taking what I studied and developing my own personal truth. My previous church experiences led me to believe there was only one truth. How would I know if I had the right truth? I was so confused. The Bible was the way, the truth, and the life. So I decided to read it again. Maybe with my new studies, it would offer some more insight—but I became disappointed. God sure was harsh in the Old Testament. That was not the God that I had been learning about. I had always believed—and still do—that the Bible was an inspired work. The original authors were indeed inspired, but what about the people who translated and wrote the various editions in print today? What were their motives, and did those motives have anything to do with how they interpreted scripture? I am not being blasphemous. I am being inquisitive. As always, I had more questions than answers, but I learned something very profound while contemplating my particular truth. I was confusing truth with doctrine. The doctrine I grew up with stated there was one truth, and my newfound insight told me that there was one truth and that truth is whatever your truth happens to be. Wow, that was eye-opening for me, but an even greater insight came to me as well.

There is a difference between religion and spirituality. My strict church upbringing just had a hard time coming to grips with that concept. I know that in these times, many people are searching for their own personal spiritual truth. We are all, it seems, at a crossroads. We are all seeing things in a new and different way. We are slowly but surely evolving a new belief system. This in itself is a healing process. It forces you to dig deep into your own psyche. You dredge up all the dark aspects of self that need to be healed. In my studies, one absolute truth has been made clear to me that helps me heal all those emotional scars that life has left on me.

We are all one with God. Every person around you that you come in contact with is one with God too. So every encounter is a holy one! This changes the way you treat people, and it also helps you to forgive people who have left those emotional scars. The peace we read about in the Bible that passes all understanding is realizing we are one with God and living in that consciousness. Therein lies the peace. Just think about it for a minute. If you treated every person you came in contact with like you would God, things would be vastly different. I'd be willing to bet that wars would cease and crime would end. Hopefully, that is exactly what we are moving toward with our newfound awareness. The concept of one truth makes perfect sense when realizing that we are one consciousness. My personal belief is that everyone has his or her own truth, which is part of the one truth of God. Our ultimate goal is to become fully conscious in this truth as we head toward being more Godlike.

I also learned that pretty much everything always works out in the end. My son ended up graduating and never regretting his decision to put himself through four years of physical, emotional, mental, and academic challenges. He will be the first to tell you that he doesn't sweat the small stuff—ever. He felt like he made it through the toughest times he had ever experienced, so nothing will ever be too much for him to bear.

I feel that way about all of my hard times. It really is true what they say, that which doesn't kill you, only makes you stronger. So if it all turns out okay, why spend time worrying? I think it is a habit we have gotten ourselves into, and it just needs to be broken by realizing when we are worrying and stop it there in its tracks. It is kind of like negative thinking. I have tried this, and it works. Every time you have a negative thought, replace it with a positive one. For example, if you are worrying about something, replace it with faith and let it go. Consistently being aware and changing the pattern will lead to a new habit of positive thinking, and we all know that what we think is what we manifest. Why manifest more worry? How many times have you said to yourself, "If I had just known it would work out this way, I never would have worried so much about it?" This kind of fear-based thinking does not serve us and wastes precious energy.

Just when I thought things were going my way, I was to stumble upon the fact that my now twenty-two-year-old daughter had met someone special and did not want to tell me. She really never shared too much with me about her dating life, and I understood this. She was a private person, like her dad. It never occurred to us that she would ever be too serious over a guy because she seemed so focused on her studies. She went back and forth between wanting to be a PA or an attorney, to the point of even taking a course on how to navigate the LSAT exams, which would get her into law school. So when she phoned me one night, it was obvious to me that something was up, but I didn't read too much into it because of her commitment to her goals. However, she sounded different. The conversation steered toward a party that she had attended. I was not born yesterday. Even though I never had any wild oats to sow, I knew the majority of college students did. She mentioned that she had met a nice guy (a.k.a. my future son-in-law), and I knew from her voice that her world had just changed. I was happy for her and could not wait to meet the man so I could make sure he was worthy of our princess. I never entertained the thought that her focus would be compromised.

I loved the days she was in college because I loved to see her so happy and I loved visiting her. We always had so much fun together. She would introduce me to alcohol for the first time in my life by telling me I needed to have more fun. I was all work and no play according to her. It was not an altogether unpleasant experience for me. She would also take me to my first piano bar, which I loved! So when her cousin moved in with her, off campus, in their own apartment, I was there to help them move in. We had loads of fun arranging all her cool girly stuff. She was and still is an organizational mastermind. She literally puts me to shame.

I will never forget, nor will I let her forget, a moment I bet she would rather bury into her subconscious. She was putting away things high up in her bathroom shelves. Her shirt came up as she was lifting revealing the prettiest heart tattoo on her hip. She realized what she had done and quickly pulled her shirt down while I stared with my mouth open unable to utter a single sound. When I found my voice, I said, "Shelley Rebecca, is that a tattoo?" She said, "No!" but quickly added very sheepishly, "Yes, but you were never meant to see it." I came to myself and realized this was a pivotal moment between mother and daughter and I needed to handle it well so she would confide in me more. I said, "Well, it's cute, I guess." We both laughed out loud because we knew there was nothing I could do about it anyway. I did not tell her that when she was ninety it would be several inches lower and would no longer resemble a heart. This was so funny, because all her life, we had drilled into her that as long as she was under our roof, there would be no tattoos or piercings. Well, I guess she was no longer under our roof.

As parents, we cannot ask anything more than for our children to be happy. Sure, I had an empty nest. Sure, I had to get to know my husband all over again and pray with all my heart that I still liked him. Sure, I was suddenly left with some time on my hands. Sure, I had to realize that at any given moment, I did not know where my children were or what they were doing. Sure, I had to have complete faith that their dad and I brought them up to make the right choices about how to spend their time. Sure, that was a completely scary thought. Sure, the house was all of a sudden quiet as a mouse. Sure, I had to decide what to do for the next forty or more years of my life. But they were both so happy, and that made me happy. All the other stuff would fall into place. It would take some time, but it would get easier. We really had done a good job with them, and now our job was shifting. We could now do what we wanted with our days. We could focus on each other after twenty years of our focus being off of each other. Best of all, we realized that the best was yet to come. What a great feeling!

CHAPTER FOURTEEN

Weddings, Graduations, and Retirements, Oh My!

She knew that this transition was not about becoming someone better, but about finally allowing herself to become who she'd always been.
—Amy Rubin

It came time to meet the boyfriend, Ben, and I made sure to lecture my husband on etiquette so he wouldn't embarrass Shelley or me. The day they visited is one I will never forget. He walked in, and I quickly liked him. He was easy to get to know, and I had no problems until I saw some public displays of affection and it was too much. I changed her diapers, for crying out loud, and he was all snuggly on the couch with *my* daughter! I bit my tongue, knowing that it would only inflame the situation. I am glad I did, because he is the best thing that has ever happened to her, and they are very happy together. I could not ask for a better mate for her. So when I found out later that they were spending a lot of nights together and practically living together, I had to constantly remind myself how much I liked him.

It was not easy, because my generation just did not live together before marriage. In my upbringing, as well as that of a lot of other people, it was considered a sin. I found myself not wanting to tell anyone and hiding that little fact from any conversation. I found out that many moms my age were dealing with the same issue, and wouldn't we all be glad when they either did it right and got married or broke up.

I got my wish when they got engaged. I got another wish when I met his mother. We met for the first time at a restaurant with Shelley and Ben. Nancy is the epitome of the Bible verse, "Her children rise up and called her blessed." She had six children that loved and respected her. She obviously ruled with a firm but loving hand. When I saw the way Ben treated his mom, any worries I had ended. I knew he would treat my Shelley with the same respect. It also quickly became clear that Nancy agreed wholeheartedly with me on the living together thing. When his mom and I got into this conversation about them and their living arrangements, I looked up at them mid-sentence, and they were both staring at us, open-mouthed. Ben gently said, "We are right here. We can hear everything you are saying." Oh boy. That shut us up pretty fast, but the point was made. I thought it was hilarious. Ben further endeared himself to us when he proposed to Shelley under the same tree where Grant and I got married. So romantic. He did it all right by asking us both for our blessing before proposing and choosing a place that was dear to our family. Okay, that meant that my year just got a lot busier.

The fall and winter of 2011 was mind-blowing for me. My daughter got married in mid-November, my son graduated from college in mid- December, and I retired in January after thirty years of teaching. All of this happened within eight weeks.

I will say that my daughter's wedding was fabulous. My whole goal was for everyone who attended to have a blast. My daughter did a splendid job of planning. She didn't hire a wedding planner. She planned the whole thing herself with me just giving my opinion once in a while as well as being a sounding board. The whole event was planned down to the slightest detail. It was going to go off without a hitch. I just knew it, but you know how there always seems to be one glitch in big events? I think it is an unwritten law somewhere.

Our glitch happened when there ended up not being any tablecloths on the tables at the reception venue. I was setting up those tables and blew a small gasket when there were no tablecloths. Shelley took charge like the little control freak I raised and promptly told the person in charge to find some tablecloths and ordered me a Long Island Iced Tea from the bar. I heard her tell the waitress to keep them coming because I was having a little meltdown. Tablecloths miraculously were located and placed on the tables, and my husband came to help me. I knew I must have been in a state when he volunteered to help me, because that meant he would be missing the big football game on TV that every man in the wedding was watching as they were supposed to be getting ready. He literally saved me, because I had to leave to tell the photographer about the pictures we wanted. He did a great job. Either that or I had one to many of those "iced teas."

The wedding was perfect. It took place in a historic chapel on the grounds of the church in which she grew up. The reception was fun, fun, fun! Everybody I knew brought me drinks, and the dancing ... well, let's just say that forty years of not being able to dance and then all of a sudden being able to brought out the long-dormant dance moves I had been piling up for the day when I could use them. My goal was realized when people said that was the most fun they had ever had at a wedding. Me too. Even better was that every single time I looked at my Shelley, she had a big smile on her face!

The next morning, I woke up, mortified. I had an awful headache and felt a little sick. Was this a hangover? I had never had one before, so I didn't know. If it was, then that meant that I must have been drunk at the wedding. No, I most certainly was not. I remembered the evening's events, right? Uhhh ... I hoped I didn't do anything to embarrass her or her new family.

As it turned out, I must have been a little buzzed, but all was well because I was assured that I was happy as a lark having loads of fun along with Ben's parents and many others who also chose to celebrate with a few drinks. Whew! It in no way was a statement about having to be buzzed in order to make it through the day.

They kept reassuring me that I'd never embarrassed them, but I still wonder. Oh well, I did not have a lot of time to ponder this, because I had a graduation to prepare for and a retirement to look forward to.

Graduation was a memorable event with absolutely no drinking involved. Matt was happy, and so was his entire family. We were so proud of his accomplishments and knew his future was bright.

Christmas came and went. I moved all my teaching stuff from my classroom to our already filled-to-capacity garage and, without much fanfare, I walked out the doors of the place I had called mine for thirty years.

I remember the day I left my campus, never to return again. I just calmly got in my car, started the engine, and rolled out of the parking lot a sobbing mess. I came straight home to a son who had moved back home after graduation. Wait! They are not supposed to come back home, right? That is the whole point of college. They spend a fortune, get a diploma and a job, and they are set for life, right? Evidently not. Luckily, he actively pursued a job and even got one only a few months after graduation.

He is now twenty-five years old, living on his own, and searching for a way to live his dream of sharing his musical talent with the world and still pay off student loans.

I am still in the process of cutting the apron strings, although it is harder with the baby of the family. I find myself searching for women I think he might like to date. He doesn't much like my matchmaking efforts, so I am trying to restrain myself. It has become somewhat of a joke between us. In my heart, I know that God has a beautiful and intelligent woman just waiting out there for him, and I can't wait until I get to meet her.

From the moment I retired, I quickly acclimated to the life of a couch potato. It went from one day running around like a madwoman and the next wondering what to do for the next thirty years. I was blessed with only being fifty-one years old when I retired, but that meant I was way too young to spend the next thirty years on the couch. I found myself at another crossroads. What was I going to do?

I decided to follow my passion. I had a secret sort of bucket list of things I had always wanted to do, and one of them was to own my own craft business. I loved to quilt and make scrapbooks and cards. I also grew up doing all kinds of stitchery, like embroidery and cross-stitch.

I had a plan. I would just spend all my time creating an inventory and then sell online or in a consignment-type shop. That is exactly what I did. I made all kinds of things and decided in the beginning to go with an existing consignment shop I already knew and loved. I moved in my corner and created a homey space for all my handmade things. I was proud of it and expected to sell everything in a short period of time. That meant I needed to get busy with more inventory.

To make a long story short, I never could recoup my time. A quilt could literally take days and days to finish, but I could not charge for all the hours I put in. Nobody is going to pay a thousand dollars for a quilt. I tried to make it up by selling more cards, which did not take as long to make. Turns out that after the economy had collapsed a few years back, people were still tight with their money in 2012, especially on the type of items I was selling. I made a little profit, but nowhere near what I had put into it in terms of time and materials. So, I hung it up and admitted defeat. It was okay with me because my love of crafting had become drudgery. It was no longer any fun. Today, I am back to having fun because now, it is only a great hobby.

Another item on my bucket list was to be a pharmacist. Well, I had tried that early on and quickly dropped out when I found it impossible to teach full-time, raise two children, and take classes at night an hour away. That's not to even mention the chemistry. Ugh! I still wondered about it and decided to do the next best thing and become a pharmacy technician. I took online classes and did quite well. Miraculously, I got a job at our local hospital in the in-patient pharmacy. I was so excited. I got to wear scrubs, and it was such an important responsibility. I loved it! I absolutely loved all of my coworkers. They were so nice and helpful. The only down side was that I was fifty-two years old and my feet were not accustomed to running literally miles around a hospital that spanned an entire city block! I tried changing shoes and using inserts. No matter what I tried, I would come home exhausted, and my feet would take a full day or more to recover. Luckily, this was only a part-time job, but I found myself resting a full day before my shift and then a full day after for recuperation. That got old really quickly. It would all end for me when I had a bizarre accident that would leave me in bed for four months.

Today, I do not regret any of those jobs I tried. I did things I had only dreamed of doing while I was teaching school. I can see the big picture now. All these experiences were preparing me for perhaps the biggest stage of my life, and that is the one I am in currently. All of my years up until now have been paving the way for me to fulfill my spiritual purpose, and I truly feel at home. I am the most content I have ever been with a job. I have focus and determination, but most importantly, I have spirit to guide me. I often heard the saying, "follow your passion and success will be inevitable." I truly believe that now. This is my calling. This is my purpose. This is my life.

CHAPTER FIFTEEN

I Will Still Want a Firemen Calendar When I Am Ninety

We're all damaged in our own way. Nobody's perfect.
I think we're all screwy. Every single one of us.
—Johnny Depp

While trying to figure out what to do with the next phase of life after retirement, I enjoyed spending time with family and friends. I questioned everyone about the deep philosophical subjects that would lead me to the epiphany I was looking for. Perhaps some of the people whom I counted on most were my mom and two sisters. I will never regret any time spent with my mom. We took trips a couple of times a year, just us girls. We went out monthly to a movie or out to dinner in town, but the trips really bring the good memories to mind. We often went to the beach to relive the family trips we took each summer. We all had to get our "beach fix" every once in a while. We would get a hotel near the water and stay a night or two.

One particular weekend, my sister Pam was turning fifty. I wanted this trip to be memorable, so I booked a bed and breakfast in the Texas hill country. The brochure said the bed and breakfast sat on top of the largest hill in the area and overlooked the valley below. I had my sister pack a suitcase but refused to tell her where we were going. My mom and my other sister Linda knew, but the birthday girl did not.

It was so much fun to tease her all the way there. I intentionally took back roads to keep her stumped. It took us a few hours to get there, and when we did, we could not get over the view. Not only was it spectacular, but the bed and breakfast was gorgeous.

It was located outside a small town known for its quaint shops. Once we unpacked, we decided to find a place to eat and then come back and get in the hot tub with some drinks. It is important for you to remember that this was my evangelical seventy-seven-year-old mother and my sisters and I, who grew up knowing that drinking was a sin. Putting all that aside, I found a package store for us and was quite surprised when nobody said a word. I had always hated beer, so I got the ingredients to make a Tequila Sunrise. The others each got some wine and beer, and we found a great deli with homemade pizza. We headed back to eat, enjoy the view, and get into the hot tub.

I was the only one of us who had ever been in a hot tub before, so the others were anxious for the experience. We had not eaten much and were starving.

Up until that time, I had never realized the profound effect alcohol had on an empty stomach. All of a sudden, things got very blurry for me and extremely funny. I was so happy! Yes, I was a little buzzed, but so were my sisters, and even my mom was unusually happy. Oh, boy! We got in the hot tub laughing loudly and unable to find my mom a place to sit. She kept trying to find the seat with no luck. She just kept bobbing around. I have never laughed so hard in all my life. It was the greatest fun ever.

We got out of the hot tub, and for the first time in my life, I had no control over my bladder. The great thing was, I didn't care, not even the least little bit. The four of us crawled up in the one king-size bed to watch a movie. We stayed up until the wee hours watching a romantic comedy and howling a little too loudly at the funny parts.

Months later, I would try to book that same bed and breakfast for my husband and me, but they never seemed to have a vacancy.

One day, I took it upon myself to comment on how good business was, and that is when I was told that they no longer used that house for a bed and breakfast. I think I know why. Oops! It was worth it because my sister had a great fiftieth birthday.

On the last trip we took before my dear mom passed away, we went to a nearby city that had great shopping. We were going to shop till we dropped. We had a great time in the hotel, as we always did. We did have our rituals, as most people do. My sister Pam could never sleep without a fan, so she took her silly box fan on every trip. It was embarrassing at first to lug that thing in the hotel lobby, but after awhile, I just laughed and helped her carry it. We each took our drinks of choice, and by this time, we were not shy about it. I, however, remained a lightweight and really had to watch it. My mom had her ever-present heating pad, and each of us brought magazines, Kindles, and other things to do in bed while we watched TV.

This particular trip, my oldest sister, Linda, had found the joy that is Facebook. She stayed on her phone, updating at every little thing. I never much bought into that hype because I didn't see the need for others to know every little thing I did. The only reason I joined Facebook was to stalk my children. It worked up until the time they blocked me. I'm not proud of it.

The last day of the trip, we were getting ready to check out of the hotel to be followed by breakfast before shopping and then going home. My sister, Pam, went to get a cart to carry our stuff. You would not believe what the four of us brought for a two-night stay! I was still getting ready, but it dawned on me that Pam had been gone a really long time just to get a cart. Linda decided to go and look for her. About the time she opened the door to our room, the hotel phone rang, and I knew something was wrong. The hotel manager was on the phone and stated that Pam had gotten stuck in the elevator, and they were trying to locate the emergency key to get it open. She was claustrophobic, so we rushed down to see what we could do.

My mom was a drama queen. She never realized it, but we knew. This woman was so loud that we literally drew straws to see who had to sit beside her in any romantic comedy. The loser was responsible for apologizing to all the moviegoers nearby as my mom would shout out loud when she witnessed the gratuitous sex that is the modern-day romantic comedy. Her drama was mortifying. When we got to the elevator, my sister was indeed stuck, but it was stuck on the first floor. It was not like it was going to crash down multiple stories to the floor. I was not worried. The management would get her out, and soon all would be well.

If you were a fly on the wall, you would have peed in your pants at the sight of us. The hotel management could not find the emergency key, so they called the fire department. My sister could be heard through the door, and she was not alone. An older man and his little dog were stuck too. I immediately thought, *That poor, poor man!* The hotel manager was trying to comfort the elevator occupants while my drama-queen mom was putting her head between her legs to keep from passing out. My older sister Linda was updating everyone on Facebook with a play-by-play and was essentially no help at all. I, on the other hand, was laughing so hard, it was hard to stop. The assistant manager came over and asked me if I wanted some wine and I said, "Seriously?" No way. Besides the fact that it was ten o'clock in the morning, I was not going to miss this for anything. The firemen that showed up had to be the best-looking firemen I had ever seen. I may have been in my fifties, but I was not dead. I jokingly told the manager to let me pick the one who would ultimately rescue my sister so she would have a better story to tell! The other manager said, "I get it now. You are sisters, and you are the bad but fun one." I said, "Somebody needs to balance out this crew."

I was so busy chatting up the firemen that I had completely forgotten about Mom. They had taken her to the lobby to calm her nerves. When they opened the elevator door, Pam cried out while Linda quickly tried to get the best picture to post on her Facebook page.

I was busy thanking the firemen while my mom was praying and thanking God for saving her daughter's life. I told my mom that there was never any danger with the elevator because it was on the first floor, but Mom would not hear it. I offered to buy a firemen calendar and even be on their subscription list. I know, even to this day, that I will buy one of those even when I am ninety.

The rest of the day was anticlimactic, to say the least. They had to turn off the electricity to the elevators, so I had to climb four flights of stairs to carry all our luggage down. Pam was in no shape after having escaped "death," and Linda had to stay with my mom. Where was she when Mom was hyperventilating? Anyway, I made three trips up four flights of stairs. I couldn't help but think this was what instant karma was like. I shouldn't have been lusting after those firemen.

When we got to the restaurant to eat a very late breakfast, Pam called her husband. Did Linda stop to think that our family was going to read her Facebook posts and worry? Of course not. I told Pam to tell her husband that she was stuck with a really handsome man and they spent the whole time discussing the latest movies and that the time passed by so quickly that when the firemen opened the door to carry her out, she hated to leave. What a great story, right? It was certainly better than the truth, which was that she kept praying to her angels, and the old man in the elevator with her kept wondering who she was talking to. She told her husband the truth. I liked my version better, but I guess they wouldn't have believed it anyway.

This was what all of our trips were like. Something always happened that was unusual and downright hilarious. I am so thankful for these memories, and when I lost Mom, I had such wonderful memories to comfort me. I wonder now what she is thinking about this chapter. I bet she is peeing in her pants, but, wait, she wouldn't be doing that in heaven now, would she? It is always easy to find helpful lessons in humorous situations. I believe that humor is a lifesaver. It is saving me, even as we speak, since I continue to care for my elderly father. If I couldn't laugh about that, I would go crazy. So find the humor in everything—or try to. Have some fun every day. Laugh out loud, and surround yourself with people who make you laugh. Hard times are so much easier to get through if you don't take yourself or things too seriously. That is easy to say when you are having fun, but if you develop that mindset, then you can utilize it in the rough times. If you can keep that lighter attitude toward the mundane daily tasks of life, you will draw more of the light into your life. I know you have heard by now that whatever you think, you attract. It is so true, but it is hard to change. It almost has to be a conscious effort to recognize those times when your thoughts are dark and change them.

This would be a lifelong struggle for me. I tended to be up and down with my moods depending on the situation. I try to not let any situation dictate my attitude toward it. I have found when I am positive, light, and in a good mood, I manifest faster and can hear my intuition more clearly to follow it. This feeling is more than enough to make me want to repeat it. It is the development of a habit. It is so worth the effort.

CHAPTER SIXTEEN

The Good, the Bad, and the Downright Hilarious

God made us friends because He knew our parents
wouldn't be able to handle us as sisters.
—*Sushil Shukla*

By this time in our journey, Kathy and I thought of ourselves as "soul sisters." We would go to classes together and meet for five-hour "lunches." One Saturday, we met to attend a wellness fair. This might be how it was advertised, but we all knew it was a psychic fair. There were many booths set up offering everything from essential oils to discounted bed sheets (for wellness?) to people giving readings. Kathy's daughter was among those giving readings, so we went to support her. As we were walking around, we saw several friends we had met in our classes. It was like "old home week," with each person having a say in what I should do now that I was retired.

While there, I decided it would be fun to get a reading. You would think I would learn through the years that when I get a whim that something might be fun, most of the time, it does not turn out how I expect. I walked around looking for the perfect person to tell me what my next step should be. Most people were booked up for the day, but my eye caught one booth with a man straightening his table. He had some items for sale, along with his readings, which seemed to be something that mirrored my own beliefs. I started up a conversation, and we clearly had a lot in common. I took that as a sign that he might be perfect to give me a reading. I would soon learn the lesson that what we think might be a sign could possibly be our own ego wanting something and talking ourselves into believing it is a sign from God. Believe it or not, this was a hard lesson for me to learn, and I still struggle with it to this day.

As our conversation continued, I got the feeling that he was flirting with me, but as a fifty-two-year-old retired female, I quickly talked myself right out of that. However, I sat down with him for my thirty-minute reading and paid him his fifty-dollar fee up front. My big question was related to my spiritual journey and my next step because I felt so woefully inadequate. I needed some direction from an objective person.

As I sat there, I thought it was a little odd that he sat facing me, knees to knees. While talking, he would touch my shoulder and arms as if to comfort me. I worried that what he had to tell me might mean I would need some comforting. I quickly squelched that feeling and tried to think of my next question and not his odd behavior because, remember, I am too old for that stuff, right?

In retrospect, this should have been the part where I got up and walked away, but hindsight is always clearer. Out of the blue, as I was considering the direction our "reading" was headed, he blurted out, "Your husband is having an affair. He is cheating on you." I did the only thing I could. I burst out laughing and could not stop! When I could speak, I saw the astonished look on his face. He clearly did not expect that reaction. So I said, "You mean with a woman?"

He looked at me like I had lost my mind and said, "Well, yeah," I said. "If you knew my husband, you would know that he is a passionate man, but his passion lies in nature. He is a full-fledged nature nerd. He will notice a pretty woman, but what will truly catch his eye will be the animals, trees, flowers, and fossils in the immediate area. If it has God's fingerprint on it, he not only knows its natural history but is also passionate about making sure everyone else understands and loves it like he does. Besides, he is so scared of STDs; he is so sure everyone willing to cheat has one. Not to even mention that he always says he can barely handle me, let alone anyone else."

I could hear this man, who was supposed to be giving me a reading directly from spirit, murmur, "I can understand that one." I knew in my soul that this was not true, but why would a psychic medium tell me something so out there? He kept on insisting that this was the case and that I should consider my options, which he clearly meant were to get a divorce.

What? I denied it even as he was insisting. We went back and forth until I said rather meekly, "I just wanted to know if I should get into this field or not." He ignored me and did what I think he thought was comforting by taking my hand and saying, "Don't worry. You are an attractive woman, and you will have no problem finding someone else that will appreciate you and be faithful."

Did he just put his hand on my leg? I guess I was in shock and couldn't see this for what it was, but Kathy saw the whole thing. She was staring at me, not at all amused.

When I tried to steer the reading back to my question for like the third time, he told me our time was up. *Well,* I thought, *that was by far the weirdest thirty minutes of my life, and did I just pay for it?* As I got up to go, I found myself wondering if my husband really was seeing someone else. Goodness knows he had always wanted me to be more outdoorsy. Maybe he found some outdoorsy and much younger woman.

Never once did I consider that this guy had been unethical. However, when Kathy approached me, she said, "What is going on? What did he tell you? I knew something was up. What's his deal?" I told her the whole story, and she sat me down and bought me a drink. My legs were shaking, and his eyes never left me, which made me extremely uncomfortable. *Where was my radar earlier?* I thought.

Kathy had a good friend that joined us, and I will say that meeting her was the highlight of my day. She was a retired, fifty-something, single female looking for her next man. She was hilarious, and when we shared my experience, she promptly blurted, as she had no filter, "That guy wanted you, so he made up a story to see if you would buy it so he could have you." I said, "My fifty-two-year-old parts? Come on; get real." She said, without even a blink, "Sharon, fifty-two is the new thirty-two. I think you need a second opinion. Go ask a friend and see if she gets the same thing."

Now that was a good idea. I didn't really believe in the "fifty-two is the new thirty-two" thing, but Oprah did, so there must be something to it. I felt flattered all of a sudden. Yes, I had recently lost twenty-six pounds and didn't look as dried-out since retiring. Not waking up at five in the morning also helped. He was a nutcase, but I was still sort of flattered.

I decided to go ask Kathy's daughter. She had a clear channel to the angels that was so accurate; surely, she would know. She found the idea preposterous. No, he was not having an affair. Who had told me that? While telling her the whole sordid story, I noticed I was attracting a gathering of other very irate female psychics. Not a crowd you want to piss off, if you know what I mean.

Evidently, this guy was making a name for himself by being way too blunt with the clients. He even told one client that she had cancer.

One of the head gals said she was going to talk to the sponsors of the fair and file a complaint. I don't know if she ever did, but I felt better knowing it would not be just my experience that would get him kicked out of the fair.

To show support for a friend in crisis, they all took me to Chili's for appetizers and margaritas. We had a blast! We drank and roasted men in general for hours. It was epic!

When I got home, I was anxious to tell my husband. I had visions of the alpha male coming out in him and he would get so angry and jealous that he'd carry me off to the bedroom to show me just who I belong to. One might say I read too many romance novels. The truth is sometimes hard to swallow. When I told him—get ready—he laughed! What, no caveman, no alpha?

He said, "That guy just wanted in your pants." Well, okay. That's a compliment, right? Then he said, "You have got to know that he was playing you. I would never do that. I would get some kind of disease." Do I know him well or what? I knew he would never. There was nothing to consider. That was pretty much how it went. My ordeal would last a whole day with much fretting and worrying and his lasted about five minutes, and that was the end of it. You have got to love men. When they are done, they are done. No extra worry or lost sleep. Stupid romance novels!

I look back on that experience as one of the funniest and most surreal. The life lessons are clear: don't believe every person who claims to be a psychic. There are unethical and fraudulent people everywhere, and it is best to beware. I also learned that I was grossly negligent in using my gut, or intuition. If I had paid attention to it, he never would have been able to tell me my husband was cheating on me because I would have left right off. Always listen to your gut feelings. They are there to serve you. If you listen to it daily, you can even base life-changing decisions on your intuition. It is that good and accurate. Intuition or gut feelings can save you from danger by warning you and keeping you safe. They can help you make decisions regarding people you come in contact with and alert you to anything going on with your children. I believe it is something to practice with and a skill to hone.

Studies have shown that top CEOs of Fortune 500 companies attribute their success to listening and following their intuition. There is always a still-small voice inside people guiding their everyday life, including making important decisions about career, relationships, and health. It is my personal belief that in today's world, people are so busy rushing around that they don't just stop and listen to that inner voice. In my own experience, at any given moment, I have so much going on in my head, it is a wonder it doesn't explode! Learning to be still and just listen has been one of the most rewarding things I have done for myself. I've heard that prayer is talking to God and intuition is his answer. The same could be said for meditation. Much can be accomplished by learning the art of stillness.

Another lesson I learned was that my self-esteem really needed another boost. It got it and I looked at myself in a whole new way, and it did wonders for my confidence. Thank you, Mr. Nutjob!

I can honestly say that while writing this book, my own lack of self-confidence delayed the submission of the manuscript. I worried about what others would think about me now that I was coming out of the "spiritual closet." I worried that I might be embarrassing my family and close friends or, even worse, letting them down. I worried that others might think I had gone off the deep end. But then I thought about how I got to this place in my life and how all my experiences had led me to this moment in time. Self-esteem and self-confidence are so important! Would a child of God be anything less than spectacular? Not by a long shot.

But most of all, I pondered the fact that I knew all of the answers I was seeking were within me already. But how did I get to them?

You have to also wonder what his lesson was. The lessons learned are not always for you. They could be for the other person in a situation, and you play a role in helping them learn it. I can only hope Nutjob decided to perform his readings on a more positive note.

The hilarity that is my journey doesn't end there. Oh no! My hairdresser and good friend, Alicia, invited my sister Pam and I to go with her on a fact-finding mission for a friend who thought she had a curse put on her. Supposedly, a woman had just, out of the blue, at a shopping mall, told this woman that she had a curse on her and she needed to have it removed. I had never given much thought to black magic and voodoo-type stuff, even though I knew it existed. I preferred to stay in the light with the angels and be happy. But I was curious, along with my sister and Alicia, and so we went. This was another "whim" I had because it was another adventure and it would be "fun." Nope, I had not learned my lesson yet.

We had a good time talking about all kinds of things in the car on the way. I took this opportunity to discuss the importance of staying in the light. We talked about Archangel Michael and all the other archangels. I gave Alicia a copy of *Archangels 101* by Doreen Virtue. I felt like the lighter we went into this, the better off we would be.

When we got there, I was shocked. It was a nice enough house, but all the houses—and I mean *all* the houses—in the neighborhood were secured and surrounded with bars. So, I guess crime was an issue? The next shock came when the lady who was to talk with Alicia about the curse took her to what I guess was her office. It was a corner of a garage with a window unit. It had a small desk, but the rest of it was like a normal garage with boxes and tools. Okay. Pam and I were told to wait in the waiting area. The "waiting area" was outside in two lawn chairs under a tree. Lucky for us, there was a tree, since it was summer in San Antonio, Texas. It was probably 100 degrees even under that tree.

Okay, this was weird. What was even more weird was that we began getting some onlookers. Cars would drive by real slow and just stare at us like we were so out of place, which we were. Oddly enough, I did not feel scared. All I could think was if my ex-cop of a husband, my sister's ex-cop of a husband, and Alicia's current cop of a husband could see this, they would kill us on the spot for putting ourselves in such a situation. Best we not tell them, then.

I began to see the absolute purest form of humor, and I could not keep it in. We both started laughing, and we did not stop until we left that neighborhood. Oh, we could tell this story, but would anybody believe us? After much talk about rituals for curse removal, we were ready to go. Thank goodness! So, we did what any self-respecting women in downtown San Antonio did: we went to eat Mexican food and drink margaritas.

When we got home, I called Linda Drake, whom I had come to respect and admire, and asked her if there was such a thing as a curse. Her explanation made sense to me. She said that there are people out there that can wish bad for others and even try what they believe are spells or curses, but the only power they have is the power that you unknowingly give to them. In other words, if you are scared to death and really believe you have been cursed, then you will likely suffer. Fear is a crippling emotion, not only mentally but also physically. It all goes back to claiming your own power. It also means that what you believe becomes your reality. I believe that if you stay in the light—meaning that all your thoughts are positive in nature and spirituality is your center—then the darkness has a harder time getting through. That was my first and last adventure into the black magic-type stuff. Alicia agreed too, and we have happily stayed in the light throughout our learning together.

You honestly cannot make this stuff up. Things happen all the time that cause a chuckle, and if they happen with good friends and family, that is just a bonus.

CHAPTER SEVENTEEN

Road Trip

Take time to do what makes your soul happy.
—Voltaire

A real blessing and a fond memory of mine is the summer my husband and I went on a road trip throughout the southwest United States during my recuperation from an ankle tendon repair. I was not able to do a lot of walking, so we decided it would just be a driving trip, which I loved to do. My husband went along to humor me because he did not enjoy road trips as much as I did.

My goal was that everywhere I went, it would be someplace that I had never seen. We did not have much of an itinerary, but we knew we wanted to go through New Mexico, Arizona, Colorado, and Utah. We had such a great time! We went to out of the ordinary places like the Meteor Crater in Arizona. We were both giddy—or maybe only I was—as we stood in the spot where all four states meet. It is called the Four Corners and is an actual spot to stand and take pictures. We took a relaxing and panoramic train ride from Durango to Silverton, Colorado, and loved it. We even went to the Grand Canyon because who could be that close and pass it up? If you want to see one of God's tremendous wonders, that is truly one of them.

While driving through Arizona, music blaring from my IPOD that I had put together especially for the trip, one of our favorite songs came on. We both loved the Eagles, and it was on our bucket list to see them in person. The song "Take It Easy" came on with the verse that says, "I was standing on a corner in Winslow, Arizona, such a fine sight to see, when a girl, my Lord in a flatbed Ford slowed down to take a look at me." I was singing at the top of my lungs, which was never pretty, when all of a sudden, we saw a sign that said Winslow, four miles. I shouted, "You have got to be kidding me! We have to go!" Even though my husband was not as excited as I was, I think he probably thought it might be cool to check it out. We exited off the highway and, sure enough, there was the real Winslow, Arizona, and downtown at a corner (just like in the song), there was a mural of a flatbed Ford with a girl in it. You could go and take your picture by it. My husband pulled the car up and let me out to take a picture. I wondered if he just didn't want to be seen with me at that point, but I didn't care. I thought this was the coolest thing! If that made me a dork, then I would gladly wear that title.

From the aliens in Roswell, New Mexico, to the sweeping vistas of the deserts and forests of Arizona, I found great joy during every one of those 4,000 miles.

Simply put, having fun and enjoying what is happening now in your life raises your vibration. When your vibration is raised, all kinds of great things begin to happen.

You don't have to go on a road trip to find blessings or raise your vibration in your everyday life. My point in all this is that it can be the way it was for me on that road trip for you too. It is my opinion that we are too busy in this world, whether we are making a living, raising kids or whatever, and we don't take the time to literally stop and smell the roses. There is a lot to be said for the small things in life. You might say that a road trip is not a small thing, but the blessings found on that trip can be found anywhere, because it is all perception and attitude.

Think of the things that bring joy to your life. Even make a list if you want to. Do something that brings you joy every day. This helps you stay balanced where you can recognize your intuition and make clear and wise decisions.

Being more observant and aware also raises your vibration. For example, have you ever been walking across a parking lot and looked down and saw a feather or a penny? Some might say these are signs from the angels telling us that they are with us always. I choose to think this, but even if you don't believe that, it will still put a smile on your face. This is a blessing found in an otherwise dull day. When I first began my journey, as I call it, I quickly realized that the more I paid attention, the more I saw in the way of not only blessings, but synchronicities. When I recognized them as synchronicities, more would occur. I believe this is because it makes us happy and raises our vibration, so more of the same happens. The key is to recognize these blessings as they come to you in your day, and that means being observant and aware.

One way to begin to be more observant is to just take it in little snippets of time. While you are alone in the car, notice the songs that appear on the radio. Do they have a message for you? Is one of them a favorite? Does it bring back a happy memory? Does it make you think of a loved one who has passed away? These are all messages or signs to which we need to pay attention. I had firsthand experiences with signs like this, but one in particular was a real eye-opener for me. Many years ago, I kept hearing the Beatles song "Let It Be" on the radio and in the oddest of places, like a restaurant and the grocery store. It got to be a joke, and I started to wonder if spirit was trying to tell me something. I had learned that when you see or hear things repetitively, it is time to pay attention. I couldn't figure out, why the Beatles? Then, one day, like a sledgehammer, it dawned on me: it wasn't the artist; it was the song, "Let It Be." I was supposed to let it be or let it go. I was a perpetual worrywart, and they were telling me to just let it be. When I hear it today, I take it automatically as a sign to look at what my thoughts are and let them go.

The same thing happened when I kept seeing the Bible verse, "Be still and know that I am God." I saw it everywhere. It was on signs, on little knickknacks in stores, and in my reading. I needed to pay attention and analyze this verse. It was like another hit on the head; I needed to be still, and what was that? Meditation. Spirit wanted me to start a meditation practice. Things like this happen all the time, but we just don't pay attention. If we did, we would see the signs everywhere.

Everyone has gifts. These are blessings given to us by God. Recognizing them is a crucial step to living your passion and fulfilling your divine purpose. One particular blessing I was given in my life was a talent of reading people. Lots of people can do this, and they may not understand what it is. I call it vibes. Did I get good vibes or bad vibes from certain people? I could tell if a person was up to no good, and I could tell if he or she was genuine. I could tell if people were creepy and if they were diabolical. What I was really doing was reading the energy of the room. More than once, I told my husband and children to not associate with a person whose vibes were negative. Everyone can do this, really. It is just a matter of being super-aware and listening to that inner barometer inside you. For example, when talking to a particular person, what physical symptoms do you experience? Does your stomach feel funny? Does your heart rate speed up? What emotions are you feeling? Sadness? Happiness? Anger? These are signs about the energy you are picking up, which is not your energy. Further along the journey, I would get sick in large groups because I would take on the energy of others, be it good or bad. I learned that this was being empathic, but I desperately needed to learn to control it. I was at a point where I did not want to go where large groups of people were present, like in the mall or movie theater. It was limiting. Actually, I am still working on that to this day. I have learned to protect myself before I am around others so I do not take on their energy. It is my belief that a lot of the energy we are carrying is not our own. The majority of it is from the people you are around the most, whether it is at home, the office, or wherever. Protection is very simple, although some make it out to be a big deal. It can be as simple as setting your intention to be protected, visualizing a shield around you, or praying with intention. When done positively and with solid intent, you will not come home with everyone's stuff, only yours, and who needs more than their own? Right?

What are you passionate about? What do you love to do more than anything? This is not random. This is your divine gift given to you by God to use in your life. You may not see a way to live your passion and make a living doing it, but with patience, intention, perseverance, and hard work, it could happen.

A prime example of this is my son, Matt. He landed a job right out of college as a MWD hand in the blossoming oil fields of south Texas. He stayed on the computer and took surveys of how the drill was operating and made a ton of money doing it. He tolerated it because he enjoyed making money for the first time in his life and he had student loans to pay off. But he didn't like it. Long story short, I see that spirit had other ideas for him. They put him in a new job he didn't like, and then they laid him off when oil bottomed out. He took this as an opportunity, and being young and without any ties, he decided to pursue music. We were all less than optimistic about his chances. Truthfully, the odds of making it in the music industry were not great for a drummer in central Texas. He never listened to the naysayers. Not once. He had already been in a band and liked the sound and the people, so he revved them up and worked like a dog to get their sound out there. Today, he has recorded several songs, and I am patiently listening to the radio, waiting to hear one every time it comes on. Are they there yet? No, but the passion is there as well as the willingness to work hard in spite of not making a great deal of money. They have new benefactors and have outlined their goals in explicit detail and are working them daily. I have to admit, I was skeptical at first, but now, if momentum stays where it is, they will have a label before the year is out. I admire his tenacity and his fierce determination to heal others with music the way he feels that it has healed him his entire life. I know what he means by this because music was my escape from the abuse I suffered as a child. It is still a haven to me. Music brings me instant joy. It is a bit like laughter. It is a quick "high." Listening to him brings me instant joy, pride, and admiration. Matt is finding a way to bring his passion to others and make it his living, even with the odds against him and friends and family trying to discreetly "talk some sense" into him. Shame on those who would bad-mouth a passion this strong. As I tell him today, I am beyond proud of him, and as long as he still is able to pay his bills, I am fine. Astonishingly, he found a job that pays well and allows him time for rehearsal and traveling for shows. I believe the universe paves the way for you if you are willing to do what it takes. If this turns out in any way other than the way he dreams it will, he will be able to say he gave it a good shot instead of always wondering what would have happened if he had only tried. Regret is crippling as we get older. As a mom, I give him space and let God do the rest.

Another way that some people find joy and blessings in their daily life is by simply acknowledging the things or people in it you love and be grateful for them. Some keep a gratitude journal, and others simply thank God in prayer. Blessings are all around us, in everything we do and everyone we know. It is up to us to recognize them and be grateful for them each and every day. Being in a state of gratefulness raises our vibration, which only causes more things to be grateful for.

God wants us to be happy because when we are, we are closer to him. We can hear his direction better, and we can help others as well. So, do what makes you happy. That could be a road trip, a passion-filled career, or giving gratitude for the blessings you recognize in your life. Whatever it is, just do it. Life is too short to be overworked, unfulfilled and without joy.

CHAPTER EIGHTEEN

No Words

❧

Take care of all of your memories. For you cannot relive them.
—Bob Dylan

Time passes by so fast until suddenly, you find yourself staring at the day you never envisioned would come so quickly. My mom loved crafts. She was a great seamstress in her younger days. She most recently loved to make cards for family and people at church. She loved scrapbooking and had many books containing mementos of her children and grandchildren. I guess I inherited the craft gene from her. During my craft business days, which included Christmas, I needed help to get enough inventory. To get ready for Christmas, I held a girls' craft day at mom's house. My sisters, Mom, and I were going to make all kinds of things for me to sell. I brought over tons of materials and instructions for what I wanted. This is when I found out that not everyone is blessed with the craft gene.

As much instruction as I gave and as much patience as I tried to convey, many of the finished products were not what I would want to put for sale with my name on them. It was laughable watching people get their fingers burned or caught up in ribbon, not to mention having to read the directions over and over again.

I began to appreciate my gift. This particular gift had seen me through numerous rough times in my life. I also considered it almost a form of meditation because I could sit for hours and not speak, whether I was using the sewing machine, cross-stitching, or making a scrapbook. My mind would wander because I knew what I was doing without having to give it much conscious thought. It was therapeutic for me and helped me to relax. Needless to say, I soon discontinued the consignment job. I simply could not make back the time I put into it. It was also becoming drudgery rather than a hobby I loved. I began to plot my next move. Moments like these were to be the last we would spend all together with my mom having fun. If only we had known.

You know how you always hear people say to tell the people you love every day that you love them. I found out the hard way that this is not only true, it is something you will never regret doing. My dad suffered three heart attacks in a short amount of time. We all took turns staying with Mom at the hospital and helping out after he came home. Shortly after he came home, my mom called my oldest sister Linda and said she had chest pains. My sister called an ambulance, and we all went to see what was going on, leaving my dad at home recuperating. As it turned out, she did not have a heart attack, but she did need to have an Angiogram to take a look at her arteries for any blockages. She went in that next morning with all of us in the waiting area. While waiting, we noticed it was taking longer than normal and wondered why, but we figured that surely someone would be out to keep us up-to-date soon.

After waiting around three times longer than average, we were briefed by the doctors. As we entered the adjacent section of examination rooms, medical personnel stopped what they were doing and stared at us. Was this normal? It was unsettling.

We were directed to an empty room, and a young doctor immediately entered the room. He was visibly shaken and sank down to the floor with his head between his knees, all the while telling us the unthinkable.

There was an unexpected glitch in Mom's cath procedure. Her vein had collapsed where the IV entered that contained her blood-thinning medicine. This meant she was not getting the blood thinner as needed. The nurses and doctors did not notice the vein had collapsed until she developed a blood clot and coded. Doctors and nurses brought her back only to have this repeat twice more. She was alive, but it was not known if there might be another clot. They took her to the Intensive Care Unit, where Mom would receive more blood-thinning medicine to dissolve any clots that might still be there.

I don't think the gravity of the situation registered with me. I just knew she was alive, and she was Mom, and moms were always there and okay. It sounds so juvenile for an adult point of view, but looking back, I think it was a coping mechanism for me. I was always the positive one of the family, and I needed to fulfill that role now more than ever because my sisters were falling apart. We began to think that maybe things were being kept secret when we got to her room in ICU and the doctors were arguing loudly enough for us to hear in the hall. We heard things like, "It never should have happened. How could they have overlooked these horrific bruises, which would indicate the vein had collapsed?" This was coming from cardiac specialists. We decided then and there to keep a log of all names and times and journal her whole stay for the next few days. Mom did fairly well in ICU, but she hated being so weak and having to have help to do everything. She even got her sense of humor back, joking with the young male nurses that they wanted to bathe her just to see her lady parts. She was eighty-three. It's funny, but we never apologized for our mom in the hospital like we did when we took her to the movies. I'm glad.

We vowed that we would not leave her alone in the ICU, so we took turns staying around the clock. My sisters worked and I was retired, so I bore the overnight stays for them. I didn't sleep at all. I mainly talked with the nurses and read. I learned a lot about an ICU nurse, and I will say that those people are heaven sent. They have a gift and are using it for the good of every patient they have. For ten days, it was grueling, but we never complained. Mom got out of the ICU and went to a room. She was still very weak, barely able to go the bathroom or move around too much, so it was decided that she would need to go to a rehab facility for a week or two to get her strength back.

The day before she was scheduled to go to rehab, we had such a great time. I stayed with her most of the day talking and laughing. She was feeling really good, and it made me feel a whole lot better. The morning she was to go to rehab, I got there in time to go with her. I found her sitting halfway in a chair, barely coherent. My dad was there, and he told me she didn't have a good night and was tired. My hackles were up; I was getting a bad feeling. I went to get the nurse to see about her night and to ask if she could rest before we left the hospital. It turns out there was no record of her night—no vitals, nothing. That did not sit well with me, and I added it to our journal.

The most important thing currently was to make her comfortable. When I got back to the room, the nurse was helping me move her to the bed when all of a sudden, my mom went limp. The nurse started rushing around to find a machine to take her vitals. The battery was dead. She looked for another machine, called the doctor, and found her blood pressure to be almost nonexistent. They called a Code Blue and told me to take my dad and leave the room. About twenty or more doctors and nurses rushed into the room to save my mom.

This could not be happening. We had fun yesterday. She felt great yesterday. What had gone wrong? I was not prepared for this at all. I was prepared for getting her settled into rehab. I lost it! My dad was comforting me when it should have been the other way around. I called my husband and sisters, barely able to speak. They all rushed to the hospital.

I knew my mom had a "do not resuscitate" (DNR) order in her file. There was no way I could make that decision. It would have to be made by my dad. A doctor came out about twenty minutes into the ordeal and said that they had been trying to bring her back, but she was not responding. Did we want to stop the efforts? I looked to my dad. We had talked about this numerous times. If there came a point where if she came back, she would never be the same again, then stopping was what she would want. That is what we told the doctor. He understood, and ten minutes later, he came and told us she was gone. I asked the doctor how she could have gone downhill so quickly, and he said he didn't know. Well, I knew. It is my understanding that she probably had another blood clot from the cath procedure that had gone wrong, which caused her death, but hospital employees would never admit that.

As I write this, I am a mental basket case. There is just nothing like losing your mom, no matter what your age. The next days were spent making sure that she had a beautiful funeral. I wrote a lengthy personal obituary that I hoped would honor her service to the church and her greatest achievement as our mom.

At her visitation, I was honored to see all the people who had shaped my young life at church. It felt like a reunion to me. It was emotional and so very good to see them paying their respects to my mom and our family. My two best friends from my childhood were so helpful to me, and it was so very good to see them. It was like no time had passed at all.

Even today, I find myself thinking that I need to call Mom when something happens I want to share with her, and then I remember I can't. I know what death is. I know she is right here in spirit. I know she is in a much better place that I can only dream about, and yet, I find it hard to live up to my own hype about how to deal with the death of a loved one. It is one of those things that is easy to tell others but hard to do for yourself.

During those times of grief, I try to remember that our loved ones who have passed are, in fact, so close we can touch them. They are just in another dimension that does not match our vibration, so we cannot see them. Sometimes we can feel their presence or get "signs" that show us they are near. We can smell their perfume, hear their favorite song or laugh when our electricity goes on the blink. I talk to my mom all the time and I know she hears me, and if I listen real close, I can hear her answer. It might not be physically, but I hear it as words in my mind. I think every loved one wants people left behind to know he or she is okay and in a grand place that we wouldn't believe. They want us to know they love us and are watching out for us. Even if they died suddenly or in a traumatic accident, they are okay. They are with God. Even if they did horrible things in their life, they are okay. They will learn those lessons another time that they did not learn while living physically.

It has been two years since she died. Those two years have been some of the hardest for my sisters and me. We consulted an attorney because we felt like we had grounds for a wrongful-death suit. When we learned that it could take years, we decided against it. I knew deep down that nobody in that cath room had missed that closed vein intentionally. I'm sure the attending medical personnel suffered with their role in her death. Hopefully, they are more careful now. Mom was our glue for the entire family, and we have been applying Scotch tape to take its place since her death. Life just isn't the same anymore. We are learning to be a family without her, and we will get there. It will take time, but I believe we will all see the value of her legacy. It is still so fresh for us, and we would all give our right arm to see her again, if only for a moment. The bright side is that we will see her again—and what a wonderful day that will be.

CHAPTER NINETEEN

And Then Spirit said, "Fall Down and Break your Leg and Hand and Tear Your ACL So You Can Rest and Focus on Your Spiritual Journey."

The older I get, the surer I am that I'm not running the show.
—*Leonard Cohen*

I heard once on a TV sitcom that God was so funny. He was such a scamp! I thought that too, and I really believed in his sense of humor and was grateful for it, up until the time I had an accident that would leave me unable to walk for many months. I had been told by spirit that I should expect a period of illness. The purpose was to allow me to step away from all my responsibilities for a bit and refocus my efforts toward my spiritual journey. I was prepared for the flu or something like that. Little did I know that a simple road trip to take pictures of wildflowers would turn into an eighteen-month recovery. It's a good thing we don't always know what's coming. I believe that was in our best interest when God set that up.

My husband and I needed a getaway, and we always loved to take pictures of things like wildflowers, animals and windmills. We would go on day-long road trips, and it would do us a world of good.

One particular day, he was off work, and I agreed to go to a nearby state park and take pictures of whatever we came across. It was supposed to be relaxing and enjoyable. We came upon a sign that advertised a waterfall. After just a short hike, we could see this waterfall. Well, that was a picture-taking opportunity. I was later to learn that a "short hike" is a relative term. To me, after being retired and not getting much exercise and having gained twenty pounds, a short hike needed to be pretty short. We set out on what was a one-mile hike. That was not too much, I thought to myself. I thought I needed to prove to my husband that I still had it in me. I could still be that girl who used to trek through the woods with him. Silly me! I managed to make it to the site of the waterfall after going down steep stairs made from the rocks. At least there was a rail to hang onto. It was slow going, but we made it. I still to this day cannot believe they actually advertised the little trickle of water I saw as a waterfall. I took pictures as best I could, since there was no real good angle, and we set out back to the truck.

I did not think this through on my way down because the way back up was daunting, to say the least. I am a very short person, and the rock staircase had huge gaps between the rocks that you had to step up and then pull yourself up by the rail to get to the next stair. One of these "gaps" was about half of my height, so it was a big pull. I felt and heard my leg snap and buckle and immediately sat down on a rock. I told my husband I thought I had just broken my leg. I felt dizzy and faint, and the world started to spin. I never did faint, but I came close. I knew I had to at least get back to the trail so I could be picked up easily by someone who could help. The embarrassment was already seeping in. I got up and made it through two more rocks when my leg buckled again, and I watched as it swayed in a direction in which knees are not supposed to sway. Talk about unnerving. I only needed to make it up one more time, so I pulled up one more stair, and my leg gave away again. I knew this was not going to stop happening, and it was really starting to hurt, so I sat down and said, "I'm done."

I have never in my life admitted defeat like that, so this was pivotal for me and also told my husband that I was dead serious and he should start looking for a park ranger. He left me to get cell phone coverage so he could call the ranger office. He was gone quite awhile, and I explained to every passerby that I was okay and help was on its way. How embarrassing!

A park ranger finally arrived and assessed the situation. He concluded that I needed to be carried out of the park back to the road. An EMS unit from a nearby town came to assess my leg before they loaded me on a stretcher to carry me out. They asked me if they could cut my jeans to get to my leg. I reluctantly said yes; they were new jeans and fit just right. However, I had forgotten that I had put on a pair of Spanx that morning. I wore them a lot due to my weight gain, even though I hated them. As she was cutting (thank God she was a woman), I saw the Spanx peeking through and quickly pulled them up, hoping nobody saw them. Again, the embarrassment was off the charts. How was I going to get through this without letting anyone know I had Spanx on? Divine intervention was called for at this moment in time.

After splinting my leg, they loaded me on one of those stretchers you see in the movies that they use to airlift people off mountains. About twenty people showed up to help. I quickly took this the wrong way. Did they think they needed twenty people to carry me? I had not gained *that* much weight. Jeez. I learned that some students from a nearby university were visiting on a field trip to the ranger office and came along to observe and help. Well, okay. That was much better. My husband, who never met a stranger, started up conversations with several of them, instantly forgetting about me except to take unwanted pictures of the trip up the hill. I glared at him, but it did no good. He said I would look back on this and laugh. I am not laughing yet, even today. They took turns holding the stretcher with about eight people holding in increments around it. They would rotate and then trade off every few feet. I had to admit it was a group effort that was carefully orchestrated, as if they had done this many times before.

We finally arrived to a waiting ambulance, and I was feeling very nauseous. They loaded me in and proceeded to take my vitals, look at my leg, and decide whether I should go to the local ER or just drive to the hospital in my town, which happened to be a level-one trauma center. As soon as we were shut in the ambulance, the three female EMTs wanted to know why I wore Spanx to go hiking. Ugh! I simply said, for like the thousandth time, that we were not going hiking; we were only going to take pictures of wildflowers. Without a blink, one said, "Why did you wear Spanx to take pictures of wildflowers?" I was mortified by this time, so I said it like it was. "I have gained about twenty pounds, and I find they really help hold it all in. I understand how that sounds, and believe me, I will probably never wear them again." Little do they know, I have not put any Spanx on since.

The decision was made to just make the hour-long drive back to our hospital since their hospital did not have an orthopedic unit. After x-rays, it was determined that they could not see a break, so it was more than likely a ligament tear. I was to rest it in a leg brace until I could see a doctor in a few days. In the months that followed, every time I went to see the doctor, they had found a new break, new bruise, or new ligament tear to tell me about. It got to be almost comical when I would come home and call family and friends. When I would tell them about my latest break, they would laugh, apologizing the whole time. What was funny was that I knew spirit had arranged for me to have some downtime. The way they went about it was unorthodox, and they sure didn't ask my opinion. Nevertheless, I didn't have a choice. The first diagnosis was that I had torn my ACL and my meniscus. I would need surgery to repair them. The next diagnosis was several bone bruises and a break at the top of my tibia. I had an MRI, and it showed the break, when the x-rays hadn't. They couldn't do surgery until the bone was healed, so there went another six weeks of waiting and barely being able to get around, even with crutches. During this time, my hand was giving me trouble around the base of my thumb. I had another MRI, which showed a break and a ligament tear there as well. I had to get a cast for one month. I had knee surgery and took another six weeks to be able to get around with just one crutch.

I can almost hear what my husband must've been thinking as he waited on me hand and foot. He probably said repeatedly, "In sickness and in health, in sickness and in health. Whoever came up with that vow never had to take care of a woman." He was my rock and never complained, not even once. I owe him big time. I was pretty much immobile because it really hurt to move in certain ways. I gained another ten pounds due to inactivity. However, I found myself doing some soul-searching. What did I want the rest of my life to look like? Big questions that I already knew the answer to, but was afraid to take that step. I don't even know the day I came to the conclusion that I was going to pursue my own spiritually based business, but I dove in headfirst. I had several courses I wanted to take to hone the skills I had been gifted with at birth. I had already started a few, and now was a good time to work on those and finish them. I could just hear spirit jumping up and down like a cheerleader chanting, "It's about time! It's about time!"

God works in mysterious ways. Sometimes, when you are not where he wants you to be, he causes things to happen in your life that make you reevaluate. It worked handsomely in my case. My poor body is still having quite a time getting back to normal. I have had physical therapy and two operations. I am finally walking better but not normally yet. I have lost some weight and have more to lose, but it is coming off, thankfully. The one thing I am not having a hard time with is my vision for my future. I see it clearly and have it worked out in painstaking detail. I have cataloged the steps and am taking them one at a time. Would I have done this if the accident hadn't occurred? I wonder. I'd like to think I would've, but I believe God knows me better than I know myself. He certainly knows what is best for me better than I do.

If you find yourself in a situation similar to mine, maybe it is time to reevaluate. If your current situation is not making you feel happy and fulfilled, maybe it is time to change and find a new direction. I know for a fact that when you put your mind to spirit-driven success, the universe smiles on you and paves the way. I have always been afraid of change, as some people are, but surprisingly, it has been easy to come to my current decisions. I believe it is because I have the full backing of all those in spirit form that are helping me. You would be amazed how this works. There are places in this book that I cannot even remember writing. When I read it, I automatically wonder how I wrote something that sounds so profound. I know how; I was guided, and the words came to me from above. I just listened and followed their advice.

How to Start or Enhance Your Own Spiritual Practice

I believe there is a fundamental difference between a spiritual journey and a spiritual practice. I personally have spent the majority of my life on my own spiritual journey, sometimes not even realizing I was on one. However, I did not fully immerse myself in a full-blown spiritual practice until my first encounter with the person I call my mentor several years ago.

If you would like to search for answers to questions you have had about spiritual topics and yearn to find the truth, or if you feel a burning need to get closer to your divine self, then perhaps developing a spiritual practice is the way to accomplish these things.

My whole goal in my journey of waking up to my divine purpose was to find out how to heal myself and others. Along the way, I have asked tough questions, read countless books, taken online courses, and attended workshops to find the best ways to live the life I was meant to live.

The following material is set up so that you can decide what aspects of spirit you would like to explore. Each modality I found helpful to me is listed with particular books, courses, and leading experts in its field. I have also included a guide of questions to assess where you are now on your spiritual path and what your passions draw you toward. I hope it helps you to begin or further enhance your own growth toward your divine purpose of waking up.

It is my true belief that every person's real purpose on earth is to heal him- or herself and help others do the same, no matter how that is accomplished. There is literally an infinite number of ways that this can be accomplished. It can be having a career in service to others, saying kind words to people you meet each day, or doing volunteer work to help victims of disaster, hunger, or abuse. It can be music that ignites not only your soul but also the soul of the people who listen, or it could be writing a book. It can be offering an ear to those who need to talk about an experience or trauma, researching and developing tools to heal others medically, emotionally, or mentally, or devoting a portion of your life to the handicapped or offering therapy to the victims of war. The list is endless.

Below is my own personal bank of modalities that I give my wholehearted endorsement to because they have proven to work for me in my spiritual growth and development. I hope they do the same for you. The list of books, courses, articles, and all-inspiring strategies are endless. These are just a drop in a bucket that is so full, we could never exhaust it. I get new information every day. Do your own research to find what inspires you the most. As I always do, start with google and just type in what you want to know, but be ready to change your life because it will happen.

The first order of business is to assess where you are presently in your basic belief systems. It is these most basic of beliefs that will form the foundation for your study and reflection. I have developed a list of questions to reflect on and I encourage you to sincerely try to answer with your heart. Maybe you will find one who needs an answer, or maybe the answers themselves will provide the focus of your practice.

- Do you believe there is a difference between religion and spirituality?
- Do you believe in a supreme being?
- What does the word God mean to you?

- Do you believe we all have a soul?
- What do you believe happens when we die?
- Does God have helpers?
- Do you believe that they can communicate with us?
- Do you talk to God?
- Does he talk to you?
- How do you know it is him?
- Did God create the laws of science?
- Do you find God and science compatible?
- Do you believe in reincarnation?
- Do you believe we will see our loved ones that have passed on again?
- Do you believe it is possible to heal yourself?
- Do you believe there is a heaven or a hell?
- What is time to God?
- What are we here on earth to do?
- Do you believe we each have a purpose?
- Do you know what your purpose is?
- Do you believe other dimensions exist?
- Are you a happy person?
- How do you get happy?
- Are you able to stay happy for extended periods of time?
- Do you consider yourself to be a positive or negative person?
- Do others like to be around you?
- Do others always seem to come to you with their problems?
- Do you feel like you are meant to do more with your life?
- Do you feel an urgency to reach out to others?
- Do you remember or understand your dreams?
- What are some ways you heal yourself?
- Do you meditate?
- What is your preferred way to meditate?
- Do you listen to your intuition?
- Does God accept everyone or only a chosen few?
- What are you grateful for?
- Are you able to find blessings during times of difficulty?

- Do you often find yourself depressed and you don't know why?
- Do you struggle with money, finding love, losing weight, or battling addictions?
- Do you believe in coincidences?
- Do you believe that coincidences can be divinely inspired?

After contemplating the questions and determining where you are on your spiritual path, see if the following modalities and strategies will help you in the process of setting up a spiritual practice.

I cannot let you start in good faith without mentioning energy and vibration as it relates to your spiritual practice. So much is said today about energy and how to raise your vibration so that you can live your best life easily and effortlessly. It seems to all be tied to this vibratory lift. I have even heard scholars say that this is our next biggest challenge in raising the consciousness of not only us as individuals but also the planet. Each of the following is known for raising your vibration.

The soul always knows what to do to heal.
The challenge is to silence the mind.
—Caroline Myss

Meditation – Of all the things I have tried and practiced over the years, meditation is hands down the most important. Simply put, meditation is turning off the physical outer world and focusing on the inner divine self with the purpose of understanding ourselves more fully as spiritual beings.

The benefits of a consistent meditative practice are numerous. There are physiological, psychological, and spiritual benefits. First and foremost, it is an instant stress reliever because deep levels of relaxation are reached. Pain can be managed better, and it aids in physical healing. It has been known to increase serotonin levels, which influence moods and behavior. It helps with focus, creativity, and vitality. For me, I was and still am astounded at the increase of synchronicities in my life that happen after I meditate. I can hear and follow my intuition more effectively, and I seem to have more patience. This is just the tip of the iceberg as far as the benefits of meditation.

There is no one correct way to meditate. It is a matter of choice made by the individual. Personally, I tried many different meditations and have my own personal preference for how I meditate each day. I enjoy listening to guided meditations or meditations with beautiful music. Some prefer to use mantras or to sit in silence focusing on a particular object. Some prefer mindful meditation, while others swear by binaural beats. The goal is to silence the inner chatter you carry with you all day and bring your focus to something specific.

Meditation does not have to last a long time each day. In fact, just a few minutes can have long-lasting positive effects on your day. Many mistakenly believe that if they have their own thoughts during meditation or they fall asleep that they have done something wrong, so they give up, thinking it is too hard. Nothing could be further from the truth. At the beginning, I did both of those things, and even today, I have days where my thoughts interrupt. I have learned to choose times to meditate when I am not so sleepy, or I make sure I am sitting up instead of lying down. It does not matter and is based on personal preference.

No matter what, I never give up on the process. A meditative practice develops over time. Just keep to a daily practice, making sure nothing interrupts that time. I love the old Zen adage, "You should sit in meditation for twenty minutes each day unless you are too busy; then you should sit for an hour." Putting meditation into perspective is the saying that we talk to God in prayer and he talks to us through stillness. That stillness is meditation, and his answers are in the form of intuition. Who would not want to take advantage of that?

A few meditations I have found helpful, especially at the beginning were guided or provided music for the focus. They included *I Am* by Dr. Wayne Dyer and *Chakra Clearing* by Doreen Virtue. These can both be found at hayhouse.com. Most of my meditations came from my studies while working toward my bachelor's degree. Many are free for everyone.

The profound synchronicities I referred to occurred after studying the Silva Method. It only took one of these meditations to hook me toward their premise of achieving the alpha state while meditating. Laura Silva has several online courses, and each includes meditations. Explore her offerings at mindvalleyacademy.com or silvamethodlife.com.

Binaural beats are helpful in achieving altered states of consciousness quickly during meditation. I went to the theunexplainablestore.com and located a few that were helpful. A lot of meditations are free online, but you just have to be ready for trial and error because some of them will not fit or work for you for various reasons. Find your own practice, and if it works, stick with it and experience the life-changing results for yourself.

Prayer – Prayer is different for everyone. Some are short and sweet. Some are right before something big and you need guidance and support. Some are in the face of life-threatening danger. Some are on your knees after a gut-wrenching heartbreak. Some are just a simple hello. Some are prayers for others who desperately need it. Thank goodness we have this venue to ask for whatever we need knowing that he knows what we need before we do.

The one piece of advice I have on prayer is that each time must come from your heart. Believe me, God knows your intentions before you do. I pray as if I am carrying on a conversation with God in my living room, only I am doing all the talking.

A prayer that involves expressing gratefulness and asks for intervention for others as well as our world is very effective and much needed. Prayers for children reach God first, or so I have always heard. I hope that is true. Prayers on your own behalf are part of why we pray in the first place; asking God for help is inevitable, and he wants to help. Be specific, be careful what you pray for, and be ready to reap the consequences of a prayer being answered the way you want. More than once, I have said to myself, "I now know what 'being careful what you wish for' means." I prayed for time away from my responsibilities so I could figure out my next steps. I sure got an answer in the form of a broken leg, hand, torn ACL and meniscus. If you don't get an answer, remember, you are now on God's timing. Your prayer could be answered now or fifty years from now. The timetable is all his. He knows what is best for you better than you do.

I personally believe prayer is a great way to meditate. Sometimes I like to just chat with God and catch him up (as if he needs to be caught up). There seem to be so many things that need his attention here.

I find it hard to pray without tears. The overwhelming sense of love I feel when talking to him is hard to describe. I also find him to have such a great sense of humor. I love it when I pray for something in the morning and I get my answer that afternoon! Belief is such a cornerstone to prayer. I know what he can do. In other words, there is nothing that he cannot do! So I pray accordingly.

One of the best people I have ever heard speak on the subject of prayer is Marianne Williamson. She even has a book of prayers. She is an expert on *A Course in Miracles* and speaks so eloquently. I love to listen to her.

Affirmations – Affirmations are a healing and manifesting tool. By my own definition, they are powerful statements used to influence our beliefs subconsciously. Positive affirmations can re-program a specific subconscious set of beliefs, challenge negative beliefs, and then replace them with positive self-nurturing beliefs. By using them consciously, you keep the positive thoughts front and center. You can spot negative thoughts easily and replace them with positive ones. Over time, with much repetition, these conscious beliefs are absorbed, and you start living to reflect your new beliefs. Affirmations work on the central basis that our words and thoughts turn into beliefs, and our beliefs, in turn, result in our experiences or behaviors.

Over the years, we pile up negative beliefs from the negative thoughts we have, and these keep producing the same negative consequences. These can be changed by replacing them with positive thoughts that become beliefs and finally the positive results we seek. It happens with a conscious effort, but the actual change takes place subconsciously. It is important that you believe what you say, and it will supercharge the effectiveness if you have a very strong emotional energy attached to them. That energy is available to change your reality. As you practice with affirmations, pay attention to the small successes as they come to you, and whatever you do, don't give up. Change does not happen overnight. I have found so many great affirmations already written that I rarely come up with my own. The queen of affirmations, Louise Hay, has a book on them called *Experience Your Good Now*. It is an excellent book on everything you ever wanted to know about affirmations and includes many affirmations for use in different subject areas. There are many websites that have ready-made affirmations to use as well as books.

I started my affirmation practice by listing two or three areas of my life in which I needed to change or heal. Then I searched for affirmations that I could relate to and that held deep meaning for me. I wrote them down and practiced saying them aloud every day, sometimes multiple times in the day. Some people put them on sticky notes and place them throughout the house as reminders, while others put them in journals or on vision boards. The important thing is to stick with it, as repetition is the key to success. In fact, don't stop saying them until they have come true for you. If you are not certain what affirmations really are, here are a few examples.

Let's say that you want to lose weight, and you are trying affirmations to help you. Each day, you would repeat these statements, however you choose to do so.

Remember, the key is to believe them and experience the strong emotions tied to them. Here are examples of affirmations you could use in this situation:

- Every day, in every way, I am approaching my ideal weight.

- I control my weight through a combination of healthy eating and exercise.
- Every physical movement I make burns extra calories in my body and helps me reach my ideal weight.
- I love the way I have put myself first by becoming as healthy as I can be.
- I love the way exercise gives me energy, helps me maintain focus, and helps me get a good night's sleep.

These are just a few among hundreds to choose from and can be found on the Internet or in books. As I mentioned before, Louise Hay is the queen of affirmations, so her website hayhouse. com is a great place to start.

Visualization – I used to teach visualization to my elementary school children to help them write stories, take tests, and learn material with comprehension. I told them it was just like taking a picture with a camera, except the picture is in your mind. I always had them close their eyes to block out all other distractions. For example, a practice that worked quite well was having them picture the events as they were happening in the book they were reading as if it were a movie in their head. It was like the book had been made into a TV show or movie. They had fun with it, and it was cute to hear all the cameras clicking out loud whenever they took a mental picture.

This strategy might help for people who think they are unable to visualize. It can be that simple for everyone. When I visualize, I close my eyes and think about the coming day and what I want to accomplish. I see the action I take to make it happen. If I am using visualization to manifest, I picture what it is I want in painstaking detail and with all the emotions I will feel when I get it. Visualization works much like affirmations because it works subconsciously through repetition and intention. It can help you influence your outer world and enhance your future so that you are living your best life.

Coupling visualization with affirmations can supercharge your manifestation. One of my favorites is by the founder of Mindvalley, Vishen Likhani. He calls it the Envisioning Method, and it can be found on his website mindvalley.com. Lisa Nichols is another great teacher; her course is called Creative Visualization and can be found on mindvalley.com.

Intention – Intention is energy. Dr. Wayne Dyer states in his book, *The Power of Intention*, "What you intend to create in your life involves generating the same life-giving quality that brings everything into existence." He details how to make this connection in his book. It is one of those books that is loaded and easy to read but deep. It is one of those books that you can reread and always find something new. I personally have not studied a lot about intention, but through everything I have read, it is a basic first step to anything you set out to do. I begin each morning by setting my intention for the day. For example, while writing this book, I set an intention for the progress I wanted to make each day. I have grown to use it when I feel like what I am going to do might be challenging. Statements of intention can be as simple as: I intend to complete chapters three and four today; or, it is my intention to have a stress-free day. You are putting that energy out to the universe, and the universe will help you achieve it. Some experts in the field even say to set your intention out loud for everything you do. It supercharges it when it is vocalized with sound. I find myself setting an intention more and more just to try it out. There does seem to be a power at work in the process.

Living in the Present – Louise Hay says, "The point of power is always in the present moment." What you choose to believe at this moment is creating your future, so the power is now. The key is to be aware of what you are thinking. If you find yourself thinking too much about events in your past, that is actually fruitless and a waste of time because it is over and done. It does not exist in the now. Likewise, if you live in the future, always thinking that life will be better when a certain something happens, that is fruitless also. All you are saying is that you do not have it yet, and that thought in itself will create a future of not having it. It's an endless cycle if you allow it to be that way. All it takes is a conscious effort to pay attention to your thoughts and keep them focused on what is happening now, and with positive thoughts and actions, a future will be created exactly the way you want it to be.

It is so easy to say this, but it is not easy to put it into practice. I am just as guilty as anyone else of thinking about events from the past or wishful thinking about the future. I believe it is not bad to daydream about fond memories. In fact, it is fun. It is just not productive to manifesting the future, but it sure can help you remember what it is you do or don't want your future to look like. Eckhart Tolle jump-started this concept with his book *The Power of Now* and has actually written several more addressing this issue as well as others. He is perhaps one of the foremost philosophical thinkers of our day. It is hard to believe he was on the verge of committing suicide when he had his "aha" moment and a new belief system formed for him. He is the poster child for finding blessings in traumatic experiences.

Manifestation – Manifesting is fun. When it works, you are like a kid in a candy store. I started experimenting with it by trying to manifest simple things like green lights and good parking spaces. I set my intention and visualized sailing through green lights or finding the perfect parking spot at the grocery store—and it worked!

All of the things I have talked about in the chapters of this book, including the power of positive thinking, living in the now, forgiveness, and setting an intention are all part of the manifesting process. There is a great comprehensive online course by Heather Mathews called *Manifestation Miracle* that covers everything in the process. Like other areas of future creation, it works by repetition and watching the sixty thousand thoughts you have in a day to make sure they are as positive as can be.

There is literally a ton of information out there on manifesting. The Law of Attraction that many people became so enamored with in the book *The Secret* only scratched the surface of attracting what you desire in your life. It is well worth the effort to study the process and can be quite fun, especially when you are able to instantly manifest. I have personally known friends that have manifested money for something they wanted; one even manifested the RV she needed for her job because she traveled a lot. She visualized it with details of its appearance inside and out. She included in her visualization the happiness she would feel when she drove it out of the lot. She put a picture of the one she wanted on a vision board and researched the different kinds so she could put a price on how much would be needed. She visited and test drove them to make an educated choice and then started a plan to raise the funds. It took a few years, but she is now the proud owner of the exact RV in the picture on her vision board.

The important things to take away from the process of understanding manifestation and how it works are that repetitive visualizations need to be done with as much detail and emotion as you can include, and you must focus on the actions you take to make it come true. Giving back is also part of manifesting. Simply put, it is part of a universal law of give and take. One can give back in numerous ways, like volunteering, donating items, or giving to charitable organizations. The charities near and dear to my heart are the Wounded Warrior Project (woundedwarriorproject.com) and St. Jude's Children's Hospital (stjude.org). Choose whatever you are able to do. It does not have to be much or cost money to do. There are endless ways to give back that do not cost a thing.

Gratitude – Gratitude naturally raises your vibration. It is positive in nature and essential to manifesting. Gratitude can be expressed in prayer or journal writing or can be spoken aloud. It has been said, "We don't always get what we want, but there are people who will never have what you have right now." That puts everything into perspective and reminds us of all of the blessings in our life. If you were to sit down and make a list of all the things you are grateful for, the list and the length of it would probably surprise you. Don't delay. We should all be thanking God every day for everything he has given us. When we express gratitude, we receive more things to be grateful for. It is perhaps one of the most rewarding and helpful pieces to any spiritual practice because it instantly brings positive thoughts. In fact, if you find yourself thinking a negative thought, think of something you are grateful for, and it will morph into a positive thought. I can say without pause that every course and book I have ever read listed gratitude as a practice to living your best life.

Forgiveness – Buddha said, "Holding onto anger is like drinking poison and expecting the other person to die." Wow—intense but thought-provoking. If our thoughts become our reality as we keep hearing, then we need to stay as positive as we can. If you are living with anger, resentment, or revenge on your mind, you have to admit, that is not exactly positive. At any given moment, you are either operating out of fear or love. Paying attention to this and redirecting our thoughts can have rewarding results. Forgiveness is a large part of that process. It literally puts a person in a place of power rather than handing the power over to someone else. It is a conscious decision to let go of any wrong done to you by another. You are not excusing their behavior; instead, you are freeing yourself from the power it has had over you.

I feel like I have exhausted this subject in this book, but that should be a clue as to how important it is, and for many, it could be an important reason they are here on this earth at this time. There are many resources out there on forgiveness. My favorite is Colin Tipping's book *Radical Forgiveness*. I think his way is the quickest way, and he even has a strategy for recognizing the need to forgive, doing so before the event has a chance to bury itself inside us and make us physically sick. Just like gratitude, forgiveness seems to be a major theme in every book or course I have studied on self-healing and spiritual growth.

Journaling – Journaling is a form of release. When you release something, it creates space for something else to happen. When you hang onto negativity, it literally eats away at you until it finally manifests itself as illness. There are many ways of releasing, but this is an easy way. If started daily, it becomes a habit, and before you know it, you are releasing on a daily basis that which no longer serves you. Wow! How great is that?

Journaling also can lead you to some patterns you didn't know existed. If you keep a journal by the bed, you can write down your dreams and eventually see a pattern develop to help you realize what spirit is trying to tell you symbolically in a dream.

Journaling can be used to keep track of people, events, and circumstances that you would like to remember in prayer.

Journaling can help you to see how productive you have been and how you might have wasted time. You can even journal the blessings of the day and how grateful you are for them.

Journaling can help you get off your chest the anger you feel over situations or toward others. Once it is voiced, it is released, especially if you go into it with that intention.

You don't have to have ten different journals for each of these purposes. You can have one journal and set it up in sections or just have a continuous session and date it. The beauty is that you set it up the way you want, and there is no wrong way to do it. Try it and see how you feel.

These are just a few of the areas I have studied, practiced, and found beneficial to my spiritual practice. There is so much out there, and it can be as complex as you want to make it. Some additional resources I endorse through personal success are:

Sandra Taylor's course The Ultimate Magnetic Power Intensive found on hayhouse.com was one of my first courses, and I loved every minute. Talk about thought-provoking; her exercises are profound and extremely healing in nature. She actually is a physicist and found the connection between science and spirituality.

Elmarie Swartz has a multitude of courses on everything from angels to auras to self-healing. Her information can be found on healing-journeys-energy.com. She has several courses on Chakra Healing and Balancing that are insightful.

Carol Tuttle is another guru on energy healing and can be found at mindvalleyacademy.com. Her course on chakras deepened my knowledge on our subtle energy body. It is thought-provoking and motivating.

Christie Marie Sheldon is one of my all-time favorites on raising your vibration. She has courses entitled Love or Above and Unlimited Abundance. She can also be found at mindvalleyacademy.com.

James Van Praagh is actually part of the reason I am doing what I am doing right now. I have read his books, taken his courses, and seen him in person. Wow. Just wow. The course I took was called Enhancing Your Intuition, and it contained practical yet simple exercises for accessing your intuitive side. I read his book *Meditations* first, where he talks about how to meditate and even has several to use. The books I liked the most were *Reaching to Heaven* and *Unfinished Business*. These were about what happens when we die. I will always consider him a mentor, even though he doesn't know it.

Doreen Virtue is the angel expert. I have everything she has ever written and have even taken a few of her courses. She covers everything you ever wanted to know about angels, including getting up close and personal with the archangels. My favorite book is *Angel Numbers,* which explains what numbers mean and why we sometimes keep seeing the same numbers repeatedly. In fact, this book stays on my nightstand because I am forever waking up at like 11:11 or 12:34, and I want to know what that means. If you are hearing or seeing numbers repeatedly, no matter where you see them, they mean something, and this book will help you pinpoint what it is. She has written so many books, too many to print here, but she can be found on hayhouse.com and numerous other websites, including youtube.

Reiki is the practice of using your hands as a channel for healing energy. There are three levels of expertise, and Reiki was actually my first experience on my spiritual journey. I took the necessary classes, and now I am a Reiki master. When I do treatments on others, pain is alleviated and energy is restored. I will be the first to make sure people know that I am only a vessel for energy and that energy goes to where their body needs it the most for it to heal itself. Reiki has long-reaching benefits and can be used for any type of energy work. It can be performed long-distance and in person. I actually found this technique after a dream where I woke up drawing symbols in my hands. This happened several times, and I would not understand them until I met my mentor, Linda Drake. Clearly, I was supposed to be using this technique. There is a ton of information out there about Reiki. If you feel called to practice, it is easy to find and get started.

Everybody knows Oprah, but if you don't know about her Super Soul Sunday programs on her network OWN, then check it out. I never miss it. It is uplifting and inspiring. I DVR all of them and watch them again and again, learning new things each time I watch. She covers all the subjects I have touched on in this book, with various experts bringing their special take on deep spiritual issues.

Emotional Freedom Technique, or tapping, is a healing modality that I feel holds great promise. It actually utilizes the same principles as acupressure. The premise is that we all have meridian points in the body that when stimulated could ease physical, emotional, or mental symptoms and even heal. EFT takes place by tapping on nine different meridian points. There is scientific evidence that by stimulating the meridian points, stress and fear responses are lessened. These responses originate in the amygdala in our brain, which is responsible for our "fight or flight" response. When we experience trauma, whether real or perceived, our amygdala responds by releasing large amounts of cortisol into our nervous system, which produces a variety of unwanted symptoms. I have personally used EFT for fear-based issues. It seems to magically erase the urgency and lessens the emotional response. I am anxious to try it on some other areas. To find out more about it, go to thetappingsolution.com or read Nick Ortner's book, *The Tapping Solution*. I believe the effects are far-reaching for this modality from helping with PTSD, weight loss, money issues, and chronic pain, and that is only to name a few. Nick and his sister Jessica offer online courses about finances and weight loss. They also host the tapping summit, which is ten days of webcasts devoted to experts tapping on various issues. I love listening to these and always come out wanting to try them.

I have already mentioned in various chapters some other books that greatly impacted my life, so here is a recap of those and some others I have found helpful:

- *Embraced by the Light* by Betty Eadie
- *The Shack* by William P. Young
- *The Secret Pathway to Healing* by Linda Drake
- *Tend to your Garden Within* by Dr. Shervin Hojat, PhD
- *The Happiness Project* by Gretchen Rubin
- *A Course in Miracles*
- *A Return to Love* by Marianne Williamson
- *Conversations with God* by Neale Donald Walsch
- *Bringers of the Light* by Neale Donald Walsch
- *Experience your Good Now* by Louise Hay
- *You Can Heal Your Life* by Louise Hay
- *You are the Answer* by Michael Tamura
- *Ask and it is Given* by Esther and Jerry Hicks
- *The God Code* by Gregg Braden
- *The Biology of Belief* by Bruce H. Lipton PhD

For those already incorporating a spiritual practice into their daily lives, there is a website that I find intriguing but deep. I have no doubt about its authenticity and the potential for impact, but some may not be ready for it yet. It is IAMUniversity.org. I have taken two courses on self-love and 100% Power, which is about gaining back and owning your own power. This is powerful stuff. That website is loaded with free things and so much information it would take days to get through the menu.

If there is anyone out there that considers him- or herself to be an empath and is experiencing actual physical symptoms caused by taking on the feelings and energies of others, then I have the course for you. It is called the Empath Toolkit by Dr. Michael R. Smith. I struggled with this, and his expert advice has helped me cope with this blessing in disguise.

Lastly, if you are being abused or know someone who is, whether physically, emotionally, or sexually, please ask for help. I have listed some hotline numbers and websites, but some are state specific, and there are so many out there. Help is readily available in this way or in the form of your teachers, pastors, family members, friends, or neighbors. All it takes is a few seconds of courage to change a life.

Child Abuse Hotline
1-800-422-4453
Operates 24/7 in 170 languages
www.childhelp.org

Teen Hotline
Crisis Text Line
Text go to 741-741
Operates 24/7 and is confidential

National Domestic Violence Hotline
1-800-799-7233

CONCLUSION

The things you are passionate about are not
random. They are your calling.
—Fabienne Fredrickson

It is my belief that we are trying to get back to our true, authentic selves as spiritual beings. We have been conditioned over centuries by man's opinion of how religion ought to be taught to the masses. Somewhere, we lost sight of who we really are. We lost sight of the greatest blessing bestowed on us, and that is our divine selves as children of God. We suffer from a blatant need to rationalize and see things as concrete. We shrug off things that are abstract or hard to rationalize as "woo-woo" and too "out there" to comprehend, let alone put into play in our own lives. My goal is to make the "woo-woo" not seem that way because it isn't. It is a simple matter of perception.

When I began to believe these truths and live them out daily, I knew I was home. It was my comfort zone, and I had been searching for that for a long time. I would have never in a million years thought I would be where I am now. My seventeen-year-old self would have me married to a preacher and hosting Bible classes for the children and women of the church. I probably still would be operating out of the fear of going to hell. I doubt whether I would have forgiven people and healed from the traumas in my life, but I also probably would have already passed away, lonely for something I could not recognize. More importantly, I would not have my husband and children and be living my dream. Luckily for us, we do not have to go it alone. Divine intervention is truly something we could not live without as we hope to progress in our journey.

Waking up so that I could heal myself and help others to do the same has led me to where I am today. It is my passion, my spiritual purpose, and my life's calling.

Everybody is on his or her own journey. If you find someone along the way that criticizes you, that is that person's own journey and not yours. Recognize it for what it is and move on. Find the truth for you, and if you feel a pull toward one particular aspect, that is God talking to you. Follow it and see where it leads.

I hope you were able to take away some cool things to help you out in your own journey. I encourage you to share any thoughts you might have with me. I welcome any and all comments and would love to answer any questions you might have. I can be reached by email at sharon.critchfield@gmail.com

The future for me entails fulfilling a dream of having my own website and blog. I plan to continue the discussion of the ideas from this book. I also offer Reiki treatments both distance and in person. I find myself at home writing and have written several e-books that will be offered on the website. There are a multitude of modalities to use when helping others to heal. My goal is to help others live their best lives, which entails getting rid of that which no longer serves them. If I can be of any help to you, I would be honored.

One with you,
Sharon

ABOUT THE AUTHOR

Sharon Critchfield is a grateful retired elementary school teacher. She taught precious children for more than thirty years. She is a proud former student of Texas A&M University, class of 1982, with a BS in education curriculum and instruction.

The next phase of her life has earned her a bachelor's degree in metaphysical science. She is most proud of her accomplishment as a Reiki master and an energy body and healing practitioner. Along her journey, she acquired additional certifications in aromatherapy and space clearing. The teacher still residing in her soul is ever thirsty for more, and she is currently finishing up her master energy practitioner certification. She is currently setting up her own website, store, blog, and private practice.

She lives with her very patient, supportive, and understanding husband of thirty-five years and her two precious dogs in central Texas.

Printed in the United States
By Bookmasters